BY MARTIN DUBERMAN

Charles Francis Adams, 1807–1886 (1961)
*The Antislavery Vanguard: New Essays on the
    Abolitionists* [Ed.] (1965)
James Russell Lowell (1966)
The Uncompleted Past (1969)
Black Mountain: An Exploration in Community
    (1972)

PLAYS

In White America (1964)
The Memory Bank (1970)
Male Armor: Selected Plays, 1968–1974 (1975)
Visions of Kerouac (1977)

Visions
of
Kerouac

Visions
of
Kerouac

A PLAY BY

Martin Duberman

Little, Brown and Company
BOSTON — TORONTO

FIRST EDITION

T 10/77

Library of Congress Cataloging in Publication Data

Duberman, Martin B
  Visions of Kerouac.

  Play.
  1. Kerouac, John, 1922–1969, in fiction, drama,
poetry, etc. I. Title.
PS3554.U25V5   812'.5'4   77–23878
ISBN   0–316–19401–8
ISBN   0–316–19402–6 pbk.

Designed by Chris Benders

*Published simultaneously in Canada
by Little, Brown & Company (Canada) Limited*
PRINTED IN THE UNITED STATES OF AMERICA

For Barbara Hart Weiss,
with love

"Well I enjoyed both Cody and Jack, many times in many ways jolly bodily and in soul love, and wish Jack had been physically tenderer to Cody or vice versa, done 'em both good, some love balm over that bleak manly power they had, displayed, were forced to endure and die with."
— ALLEN GINSBERG, from the introduction to Kerouac's *Visions of Cody*

"One lives by memory . . . and not by truth."
— STRAVINSKY

Characters

(in the order of their appearance)

CAMERON	EVELYN POMERAY
JACK KEROUAC	EMIL KEROUAC
WOMAN IN AUDIENCE	GABRIELLE KEROUAC
JOHN WIMAN	TRISTESSA
CONRAD CARVER	JAPHY RYDER
ALLEN MOORE	SIMON
IRWIN GOLDBOOK	CACOETHES
RAPHAEL URSO	PRINCESS
RUTH HEAPER	TIMMY POMERAY
WILL HUBBARD	TV CREW MEMBER
CODY POMERAY	JOEY ROSE
MARYLOU POMERAY	STELLA KEROUAC
STATE TROOPER	

Author's Note

Visions of Kerouac is an amalgam of my words and Jack Kerouac's. Some events are wholly imagined, much of the dialogue is invented, certain characters are composites; I've aimed at truth of mood, not truth of fact. The play is a meditation on Kerouac's life — much as his book *Visions of Cody* is a meditation on Neal Cassady's.

I've retained the names Kerouac himself used in his printed work for most of the important people in his life.

Whenever Kerouac's own words appear in the play, they do so with the permission of the Kerouac estate.

To curtail costs, the author encourages the double-casting of smaller roles. For example, actors in the TV debate (act one, scene 1) could later double as the STATE TROOPER, SIMON, JOEY, TV CREW MEMBER, et cetera.

Production History

An early version of the play was given a staged reading at The New Dramatists, New York City, in June 1976. A later version was performed in work shop at The Lion Theater Company, New York City, in December 1976.

Act One

SCENE 1

TV sound stage, New York City, 1958. In the middle of a station break.

Those on stage include: CAMERON, *the moderator — youthful, bland, bright;* CONRAD CARVER, *an English novelist — about forty, pudgy, elegantly mannered, witty;* JOHN WIMAN, *around forty-five, prototypical Jewish liberal — articulate, impassioned, aggressive;* ALLEN MOORE, *Professor of Anthropology — soft-spoken, polite, well-intentioned, a little vague;* JACK KEROUAC — *a handsome, stocky man in his mid-thirties, wearing a checkered-plaid shirt, wrinkled pants, lumberjack boots.* HE *carries a large Dixie cup in one hand.*

CAMERON: *(Under, to* KEROUAC*)* — Mr. Kerouac, if you'd resume your seat, please . . . we're about to go back on the air . . .

KEROUAC: Huh? . . . Oh yeah, sure . . .
(A WOMAN IN AUDIENCE *rises from first row and holds up an autograph book for* KEROUAC *to sign)*

WOMAN: Mr. Kerouac, I wonder if you would . . .

3

KEROUAC: *(Smiling)* — oh sure, sure . . .
 (HE *signs autograph*)

CAMERON: Mr. Kerouac — we're about to go on the air again —
 (KEROUAC *sits. Lights up full*)

CAMERON: *(Out to audience)* Welcome back to "News-makers." We've been discussing tonight Jack Kerouac's new novel, *On The Road,* which seems on its way to becoming *the* literary event of 1958. Just before the break, one of our distinguished panel members, Mr. Wiman, made the point that —

KEROUAC: *(Interrupting, sarcastic)* — our distinguished political columnist John Wiman — otherwise known as *Broadway Sam,* Showbiz city slicker —

WIMAN: — now just a minute, Mr. Kerouac!

KEROUAC: — divorced from the folkbody blood of the land —

WIMAN: — exactly what the Nazis said!

KEROUAC: — rootless, tho permissible fools, who really don't know how to go on living —

CAMERON: — gentlemen, gentlemen! — *please!*

CARVER: *(Arch) Do* tell us about your rootedness, Mr. Kerouac. I'd be genuinely interested. It's hardly a style one associates with being "on the road."

KEROUAC: That tone, Carver . . . that's my chief complaint about the contemporary world you all inhabit so easily: the facetiousness of "respectable" people . . . destroying old human feelings — older than *Time* magazine . . .

CAMERON: Mr. Moore, do you —

4

CARVER: — that seems a remarkable turnabout. I associate the *Beats* with disdain for the "old human feelings," and now you talk reverently about retaining them . . . I must say, Kerouac, I don't find your "vision" very — uh — *steady*.

WIMAN: Your people care deeply about one thing: *not* caring. It's the cult of *un*-think: asocial, apolitical, amoral.

KEROUAC: Well, walking on water wasn't built in a day . . .

WIMAN: I came here to have a rational discussion of the —

KEROUAC: — you wanna talk about the futility of Surrealism? That's always a good one. Or how about the loveliness of Mozart's flute? Who do you think the best jockey in America is today? Hah? And you betta say Turcotte!

CAMERON: Perhaps if we could —

WIMAN: *(Angry)* — our society faces two *serious* questions, Mr. Kerouac —

KEROUAC: — Jack, Sam, Jack —

WIMAN: — two questions that responsible, rational human beings are addressing themselves to: something called the hydrogen bomb — I trust you've heard of it —

KEROUAC: — oh yass, yass indeed — part of what Irwin usta call the "Nickel-O Syndrome," back in the early forties when we were at Columbia.

MOORE: The Nickel-O?

KEROUAC: A bar across the street from where Irwin lived in the East Village. Neon lights and cast-offs —

WIMAN: — and the *second* question is one of human equality, as exemplified by the current struggle among Negroes for civil rights. *These* are the dominant issues of our time.

KEROUAC: When God says "I Am Lived," we'll have forgotten what all the shoutin' was about.

CARVER: Oh my — aspirations of high piety. Much on the order of Billy Sunday. But I'm surprised, Jack —

KEROUAC: — Mr. Kerouac —

CARVER: — surprised that you seem to have lost your well-publicized enthusiasm for esoteric Eastern religions.

KEROUAC: "Beat" is like Saint Francis . . . a still center . . . an open heart . . .

CARVER: Ah — William Blake's little Lambs, eh? "To see a World in a Grain of Sand/And a Heaven in a Wild Flower."

KEROUAC: On your lips Blake sounds like donkey piss.
(TV monitor bleeps)

CAMERON: The view Mr. Wiman is trying to express, Jack, is one commonly held among people who consider themselves political activists.

KEROUAC: *(Growling)* Don't give me that shit.
(TV monitor bleeps)
I'll just walk my ass —
(TV monitor bleeps)
— right outta here . . .

WIMAN: As a political columnist, I have to write about Dwight D. Eisenhower every week —

KEROUAC: — he's very witty —

WIMAN: — you interrupted me.

6

KEROUAC: Education is education.

WIMAN: For a man who claims to value kindness, you're not very polite.

KEROUAC: I'm polite, I'm not *politic*. You came here tonight to attack me!

CARVER: We came here to try to understand you. But I have to say, with due respect, Jack —

KEROUAC: — *Mr.* Kerouac —

CARVER: — that you don't make the task very easy.

KEROUAC: Why? Because I'm drunk?
    (TV monitor bleeps)
Because I believe in ecstasy of the mind?

CARVER: *(Dry)* Because you seem to have no idea *what* you believe. Or if you do, you have limited ability to communicate it.

KEROUAC: *(Suddenly yelling)* I'm gonna put you in a horseshoe and give you to a horse to wear in the Battle of Chickamauga!

CAMERON: Gentlemen, gentlemen, please! Ours is, after all, a forum devoted to rational —

KEROUAC: *(Still yelling)* — while you're alive on earth the very hairs of your cats on your clothes are blessed — that's what I believe! What do you believe in, hah, Wiman?

WIMAN: It's clear you haven't heard a word I've said —

7

MOORE: (Overlapping KEROUAC) . . . such behavior is perhaps . . . a signal of distress . . . a cry for love, even . . .

KEROUAC: (Continuing) You get published *every week*, huh, Wiman? Try waitin' *eight years* and see what it does to your hearing!

WIMAN: What I believe in, Mr. Kerouac —

CAMERON: Gentlemen! Gentlemen!

KEROUAC: — yeah, whaddaya believe, Wiman, whaddaya believe? . . . you tell me what you believe, I wanna know what you believe in —

WIMAN: — if you'll allow me to finish my sentence —

KEROUAC: — we're all in *Heaven,* that's what I believe — live your lives out . . . love your lives out . . .

(KEROUAC *goes off-camera for liquor bottle*)

CARVER: (*Almost as an aside*) As I said: furtive sexuality plus confused aspirations of piety.

WIMAN: (*"Dignified"*) If I might be allowed to finish a sentence . . . *I believe* in the capacity of human intelligence to change society, to create a world in which there is justice, freedom, love —

KEROUAC: (*Yelling from offstage*) — oh yeah, I'll vote for love!

WIMAN: We have to *fight* for that kind of world —

8

KEROUAC: *(Returning) Fight* for love?!

WIMAN: You and your friends are trying to destroy this generation's instinct to *care* about the world.

KEROUAC: I'm sure the cherubs are grateful for the dignity of those words.

CARVER: *("High-toned")* I find it astonishing to hear such flip, infantile remarks. Fortunately, the Boris Pasternaks of the world still live. Fortunately —

KEROUAC: — whadda you know about the world? — negative little paper-shuffling prissy —	CAMERON: Gentlemen! Gentlemen!
KEROUAC: — who are these men that insult men, these people who wear pants and sneer? What makes you all so clever in a meat grinder?	CAMERON: — Mr. Kerouac, really! I think perhaps we may —
	MOORE: — Mr. Cameron . . . uh, if I may, Mr. Cameron —

CARVER: — vulgar ravings, nothing more —

CAMERON: — perhaps if we proceed somewhat more systematically —

MOORE: — as I've been trying to say, there are many ways, different ways, to be responsible to justice and love.

WIMAN: Responsibility means struggle.

KEROUAC: What are all your "decent" plans for "social change" when *you're ignorant of your own broken hearts?*

WIMAN: — self-indulgence — a convenient excuse for passivity, for selfish —

KEROUAC: — go to the lone plateau where you can hear the zing of *silence* — the sound *of your broken hearts! That's* what "Beat" means, beaten down to a nakedness where you're able to see, you're deranged enough to see that the mind of nature is *intrinsically* insane! When will Billy Graham admit it?

CARVER: *(To* CAMERON*)*
Really, Cameron, I think this "exhibition" has gone far enough.

KEROUAC: *(Ignoring him)*
— No, you rather blame all troubles on a government or a secretary of state or a white racist, lay the blame on such born victims of birth as that! Just 'cause you got white skin and ride in the front of the bus don't make you suffer less!

CAMERON: Yes, quite . . .
Mr. Kerouac — Jack —
I'll have to ask you —

WIMAN: *(Sardonic)* In short, nothing, nothing can be changed. All equally guilty, equally helpless.

KEROUAC: I'll personally bullwhip the first bastard
(TV monitor bleeps)
who makes fun of human hopelessness!

CARVER: I think I've heard sufficient nonsense for one evening.

MOORE: What Mr. Kerouac is saying is that if there's *always* an emergency — and there always is — it implies the danger is internal as well as external.

WIMAN: Which is precisely why we need human courage.

KEROUAC: *(Imitating W. C. Fields)* Um, yes, Jackson m'boy — human courage, the opiate. But opiates are human too. If God is an opiate so am I. Therefore, *Mister* Wiman — *eat* me. We'll all laugh at the Second Coming!

CAMERON: *(Jumping in)* I want to thank our guests for joining us this evening on "Newsmakers" . . .

CAMERON: The subject under discussion tonight was "Is There A Beat Generation?"	KEROUAC: *(Out to audience)* "Is there a world?"*

(The lights dim on CAMERON *and the panelists)*

CAMERON: *(his voice gradually fading)* We were pleased to have as our guests tonight, Mr. Jack Kerouac, author of the best-selling novel *On The Road,* already the subject of lively controversy;	CARVER: *(Overlapping)* . . . barbarian antics . . . MOORE: *(Overlapping)* . . . *jongleurs* of the twentieth century . . . WIMAN: *(Overlapping)* I had hoped for some civilized dis-	*(As* CAMERON *begins windup, Kerouac moves drunkenly down to edge of stage, starts yelling out at audience over Cameron's concluding remarks)*

CAMERON: *(continuing)*
John Wiman, political columnist and well-known civil libertarian; Professor Allen Moore of New York University, author of *Primate Cultures: An Ethnographic Inquiry* . . .
(Voice now inaudible, lights on panel out)

WIMAN: *(continuing)*
course, but apparently we've wandered into a downtown bar.

KEROUAC: I go claim the bloody dolmens of Carnac, go claim the Cornish language of Kernuak, little cliff-castle at Kenedjack in Cornwall, or Cornouialles itself near Quimper and Keroual . . .
(Peering out at audience)
Whoo . . . I'm the Phantom of the Opera, folks . . .

(KEROUAC, in a spot, totters on the edge of the stage. TV CREW starts to strip set, silhouetted behind him)

KEROUAC: . . . Call themselves poets
Call themselves Kings
Call themselves Free
Call themselves
　　Hennis free
Calls themself . . .
Calls themself *catshit!*
Calls themself me . . .

(Pause)

12

What am I doin' here? . . . Is there some way I'm *supposed* to feel? . . .

(Spot dims on KEROUAC*)*

IRWIN: *(Voice-over)* — Jacky! Jacky! You've *got* to come down from your character heights!

(Spot out. KEROUAC, *in darkness, does some quick visual change [for example, turning his jacket inside out to reveal the letters* COLUMBIA] *to suggest — when lights go up in scene 2 — that the time has shifted from 1958 to 1944)*

KEROUAC: *(Voice-over)* Huh? Who's that? Irwin? Is that you, Irwin?

IRWIN: *(Voice-over)* Of course it's me! And you've got to decide *now*, Jacky, what you're going to do with your life! You hated the Merchant Marine, you won't come back to Columbia, you —

KEROUAC: *(Voice-over)* — now listen, little Irwin —

SCENE 2

Lights up on IRWIN's *apartment, 1944.*

The apartment is filthy, cramped; cushions and mattresses are scattered on the floor. A sign is tacked over the stove: WE JELL PLOTZ. *Onstage with* KEROUAC *is* IRWIN — *about twenty, short-haired, clean-shaven, intense, hyperverbal, brilliant, given to sudden shifts of mood from mournful to manic — but with his essential sweetness and generosity always showing through.* HE *looks like one of the Three Stooges — the tender, lovable, vulnerable one. Also present are:*

RAPHAEL URSO — *in his early twenties, he looks and often acts like an Italian Dead End Kid; given to wild flights of lyrical fantasy, bursts of fury; always horny; usually unpredictable.*

RUTH HEAPER, KEROUAC's *girl friend — a pretty brunette, also in her early twenties; warm, good-natured.*

14

WILL HUBBARD — *pale, lanky, laconic; about ten years older than the others.*

IRWIN: Jacky — the days of wrath are coming! It's 1944 — there's a war on! And all *you* want to do is bum around the country, looking for hincty sweets on village greens. *Believe me,* I know what's best for you — you've got to *stop reading Thomas Wolfe!*

KEROUAC: Irwin, how annoying you do get.

RAPHAEL: He's right. Read more Céline, *all* Dostoevsky!

IRWIN: — let me talk!

KEROUAC: *(Amused)* When *don't* you, little Irwin?

RAPHAEL: Funny *ex*-halfbacks end up selling Pepsi-Cola.

IRWIN: Jack, I specifically asked Will to come over to-night to — *(Turning to* WILL HUBBARD*)* Will — *please* explain to Jack that —

HUBBARD: *(Laconic)* — later, later, Irwin. Talking can ruin a good high.

RAPHAEL: *(Growling at* HUBBARD*)* No-good Times Square junkie freak!

HUBBARD: We all have our visions, Raphael.

IRWIN: Don't mind Raph. Deep down he's very gentle.

HUBBARD: I hope you make it to the bottom alive. I've read his poetry.

RAPHAEL: You hot-blooded Anglo-Saxons! I'm gonna get you gang-raped, Hubbard, open up that ass of yours!

HUBBARD: Splendid! Perhaps we can get the same gang to close your mouth.

RUTH: This is the crowd that's going to save American literature?!

15

IRWIN: World literature! We have a Blakean message for the Iron Hound of America!

RUTH: I'm sorry! I'm sorry!

HUBBARD: So are Van Doren and Trilling.

IRWIN: *(With mounting fervor)* How can the East have any respect for a country that has no prophetic Poets? The Lamb of America must be raised! Big trembling Oklahomas need poetry and nakedness!

KEROUAC: *Now* you're talking!

IRWIN: *(Somewhat annoyed at being interrupted)* Dilly-dallyers in offices have to have somebody give them a rose! *Wheat's got to be sent to India!*

RAPHAEL: Enough, enough! I gotta get laid!

IRWIN: Raphael — shut up!

RAPHAEL: Wanna buy a necktie with hand-painted gravy stains?

RUTH: Is this what they mean at Columbia by "deep form"?

IRWIN: Ruthie, you *must* understand that we *(Gesturing grandly to include everyone)* — *We* — are revolutionizing American literature!

RAPHAEL: Yeah? — well I may give up the poetry racket altogether, paint religious mural for Mafia bars. *(Yelling)* I wanna heart-shaped moat like Dali's! Triplex pigeons on the roof! A villa on Capri!

IRWIN: You see, Raph — you write a poem every time you open your mouth.

RUTH: *(Mimicking IRWIN)* "You are a great prophetic bard!"

16

IRWIN: New hip classical doll scenes will take place in the Port Authority or the Seventh Avenue toilet —

KEROUAC: We'll lead schools in exile: We'll —

RUTH: *(Getting ready to leave)* — wonderful. Unfortunately, *we* have to get to the Laundromat before it closes.

KEROUAC: *(To RUTH)* Aw, c'mon, babe . . . put on the Hawk . . . have another beer . . . Wanna beer, Will?

HUBBARD: Nothing for me . . . uh, unless you have a little codeine cough syrup?

RAPHAEL: How about a dozen suppositories!

RUTH: Jack, let's go . . . please . . .

RAPHAEL: *(To RUTH and KEROUAC)* Are you two gonna make it tonight or not? I gotta know.

HUBBARD: Which two? This is rather a mixed crowd . . .

IRWIN: You're too corporeal, Raphael. *(To RUTH)* Ruthie, I *have* to talk to Jack . . . so many complex, interesting and illuminating things have happened while he's been away.

RUTH: You've been talking his ear off for *hours!*

KEROUAC: *(To IRWIN)* I can come back tomorrow.

IRWIN: This is *urgent! Very* serious!

KEROUAC: *(Throwing up his hands as if helpless to resist)* I forgot how crazy New York is — nobody does anything but sit around and *talk* . . . *(To RUTH)* I'll call you later, hon . . .

RUTH: *(Angry, heading toward the door)* I've hardly talked to you since you've been back! My shrink's right — you take advantage of my good nature.

KEROUAC: Aw, that asshole shrink just wants to get in your pants.

IRWIN: No fighting! No fighting! You're all wonderful people — and great writers!

RUTH: Don't be compulsive about loving everyone, Irwin. It shows a lack of discrimination. *(To* RAPHAEL*)* Drop me off, will you, Raph?

RAPHAEL: *(With mock Groucho Marx leer)* Dee-*light*-ed, my dear!

RUTH: *(To* KEROUAC*)* Let me know when my turn comes around again.

KEROUAC: I'll callya later, hon. I promise . . .

RUTH: I won't hang on it. *(*SHE *exits)*

IRWIN: *(Calling after her)* Don't worry! The sunflowers are going to be surrounded by *millions* of suns!

RAPHAEL: *(To* KEROUAC*)* You're making a big mistake. Her legs are pure affection.
   *(*RAPHAEL *starts to leave)*

IRWIN: *(To* RAPHAEL*)* And where are you going?

RAPHAEL: To lay Ruth, of course. Then I'm gonna hang out. Waiting on the street corner for no one — *that's* true power!
   *(*HE *exits)*

IRWIN: Will, *why* haven't you been talking more? Jack *has* to decide what he's going to do with his life, and you're the *only* person who can tell him. *(*HE *pauses)* Will — *tell* him!

HUBBARD: Tell him *what?*

IRWIN: I showed you a chapter of his novel.

18

KEROUAC: *(Startled)* You did? *(To* HUBBARD*)* Whaddya think of it?

HUBBARD: Good, good . . .
    (Pause)

KEROUAC: But whaddya think of it . . . specifically?

HUBBARD: *(Pursing his lips)* Why . . . I don't specifically *think* of it. I just rather like it, is all.

KEROUAC: *(Hurt)* Well, it was fun writing it.

HUBBARD: I daresay . . . Now tell me — how would I get papers if I wanted to join the Merchant Marine?

IRWIN: *(Astonished)* Join the wha—?

HUBBARD: Shush, Irwin . . . so much need to be noticed . . .

IRWIN *(Pouting)*: I don't care . . .

HUBBARD: Of course you care. You care too much. *(Turning to* KEROUAC*)* Do answer my question. *(Looks at his watch)* Mary's waiting for me in the apartment. *(Beaming)* We found a new doctor. Got *two* prescription pads. Now about the Merchant Marine . . .

KEROUAC: What was your last job?

HUBBARD: Bartender in Newark.

KEROUAC: Before that?

HUBBARD: Summons server in Newark. Exterminator in Chicago. Of bedbugs, that is.

IRWIN: *(Breathless)* Will married a White Russian countess in Yugoslavia to get her away from the Nazis.

HUBBARD: And I held up a Turkish bath in Chicago — almost.

19

KEROUAC: Almost?

HUBBARD: I got distracted.
(IRWIN *giggles*)

KEROUAC: Well . . . you get your Coast Guard pass first, down near the Battery . . .

HUBBARD: Precisely *where* near the Battery?

IRWIN: Will hates confusion.

HUBBARD: Also liberals and cops. (*Charming smile*) You see, I'm really a Kansas minister.

IRWIN: (*Adoring*) *Tell* us about it, Will. *Please!*

HUBBARD: Irwin, do let Jack talk.

IRWIN: Jack doesn't like to talk.

HUBBARD: (*To* KEROUAC) Very sensible of you. 'Tis a finkish world. (HE *gets up*) Go to the movies a lot. And don't let Irwin bother you with *literary* matters. I'll give you a bang of morphine — much better for you. Read only Spengler. He will EEE-di-fy your mind, my boy, with the grand actuality of *Fact.*

KEROUAC: (*Shrugging*) The grit's the same everywhere.

HUBBARD: What on EARTH do you mean? Really you're awfully funny . . . *My* life is perfectly free of grit. *Because* I pay attention to Fact, to how things *are*, not how they "should" be . . .

IRWIN: (*Grandiloquent*) Grit blows in the endless dust of atomic space!

HUBBARD: My Gawd — you *will* be literary! I'm not going to stay another minute. Why, when I was your age —

KEROUAC: — how old are ya?

HUBBARD: Thirty-two.

KEROUAC: You're only nine years older than me.

HUBBARD: But I'm an agent from another planet. Unfortunately, I haven't gotten my orders clearly decoded yet. . . . Well, must fill some new prescriptions . . .

IRWIN: Be careful, Will — you'll get in trouble.

HUBBARD: Always careful. Unlike the riffraff.
(HE *exits*)

IRWIN: *(Calling after him)* When will I see you —?

HUBBARD: *(Offstage)* Soon . . .
(IRWIN *comes back into room*)

IRWIN: *(To* KEROUAC*)* Do you realize *everyone* we know is a genius? Especially Hubbard.

KEROUAC: You think all your friends are geniuses.

IRWIN: Hubbard is *uber*-genius! He knows *exactly* what's happening. *(Gesturing toward window)* . . . the great canvas of disintegration . . . I'm using these symbols in a new poem, incidentally —

KEROUAC: — Irwin?

IRWIN: — Jack, if you go on interrupting me, how will you ever understand what's going on? Come here! *(*HE *pulls* KEROUAC *over to the window. Pointing out triumphantly)* Look at that!

KEROUAC: At what? . . .

IRWIN: The big sign blinking "Nickel-O." That's *it!* The place has *everything* — all the cast-offs with nothing to do at four in the morning but stay there, sheltered from the darkness . . . I *have* to take you!

KEROUAC: *(Kidding)* My Ma and Pa say you're gonna destroy me.

IRWIN: *(Pleased)* Really? Aren't they sweet! How about all the people who want to destroy *me?* But I keep on leaning my head against the bridge.

KEROUAC: What bridge?

IRWIN: Any old bridge. I'm not fighting with God . . . *(Peering out at the sign)* See how bright the lights are! *Nickel-O! (Enjoying himself enormously)* The bluish neon illuminates every pore, you see monstrous blemishes, great hairs sticking out of moles. Everybody looks like a *geek!*

KEROUAC: The world isn't as sad as *that* . . . it's the war and everything . . .

IRWIN: It's a medieval plague! Only this time it will ruin everything, don't you see?

KEROUAC: Stop asking me that! No, I don't see.

IRWIN: You will — eventually. It's the great molecular comedown. All character structures based on tradition will slowly rot away, people will get the hives right on their hearts, great crabs will cling to their brains . . .

KEROUAC: *(Nervous laugh)* You're goofing . . .

IRWIN: Marijuana fumes will seep out of the Stock Exchange. College professors will suddenly go cross-eyed and start showing their behinds to one another.

KEROUAC: Irwin, why don't you go back to becoming a radical labor leader, like you always wanted?

IRWIN: Hubbard will help you see it. He's helped me see *everything.* Of course he *loves me.* . . . *That's* what I have to talk to you about, *very* important! Let's have dinner at the Nickel-O.

KEROUAC: That's enough, Irwin, I gotta go.

IRWIN: *Now?* You're leaving *now*, just when I was —

KEROUAC: Irwin — I got things to do, places to go! I didn't quit Columbia to sit around all day and *talk!*

IRWIN: It's true you're not very good at it . . .

KEROUAC: I wanna see where the rest of those lights on the highway stretch to! Prowl and roam, study the real America!

IRWIN: *Stop* spouting that Thomas Wolfe romantic posh! Next it'll be one of your speeches about those happy-go-lucky Americans you pretend to see everywhere.

KEROUAC: (*Gesturing out of the window toward the Nickel-O*) Better'n seeing zombies everywhere . . .

IRWIN: Don't you realize I also believe in the possibility of human love at the ends of the night?

KEROUAC: (*Big smile*) I believe in it every *morning*. Now c'mon, I gotta find Ruthie . . .

IRWIN: Jack, are you in love with Ruth?

KEROUAC: Huh?

IRWIN: Stop acting like you don't understand the language! Those Canuck "huhs" only work in *polite* society.
(THEY *laugh*)

KEROUAC: I like Ruthie, yeah. She's a good kid.

IRWIN: Then why do you mistreat her?

KEROUAC: Do I?

IRWIN: You won't *connect*. You keep veering off —

KEROUAC: Stop analyzing me. You're like the priests in high school.

23

IRWIN: *(Giggling)* I'm a black monk. Raphael says so.
   (THEY laugh. Pause)
   (Deeply felt) Jack — I love you.

KEROUAC: *(Perfunctory)* I love you, too, Irwin.

IRWIN: No, I mean: I *love* you.

KEROUAC: Awww, Irwin . . .

IRWIN: I love you and I want to sleep with you, and I
   really like men, and that's part of what's changed, and
   I — *(Takes a deep breath)* and I want to sleep with
   you.

KEROUAC: *(Confused, sad)* Oooooooh, no . . .

IRWIN: I don't mean *now,* or tomorrow . . . there's no
   hurry, things happen . . . I just wanted to let you
   know . . .

KEROUAC: But you know how much I like girls, Irwin . . .

IRWIN: Of course I do. And I respect that. Just as *you*
   accept *my* soul with all its throbbings and sorrows
   and —
   *(A sudden shaft of light as the apartment door
   opens. A young man — CODY — is silhouetted in it)*

IRWIN: Hello . . . Who are you?

CODY: Hunkey gimme this address. Said to come here
   when I got in from Denver. *(Peering in KEROUAC's
   direction)* That you, Hunkey?

KEROUAC: I'm Jack.

CODY: Oh . . . whaddaya say, Jack!

IRWIN: I haven't seen Hunkey in months . . . I'm Irwin.
   Do you want to come in?

CODY: Sure — no place else to go.
(HE *pulls a young girl into the light*)
This here's my wife, Marylou.

IRWIN: Marylou . . . that's a nice name.

MARYLOU: Yeah? I don't like it . . . common.

IRWIN: Well come on in. We got lots and lots of room.
We're a cornucopia of roomy rooms.
(MARYLOU *giggles*)

CODY: Appreciate that.
(THEY *close the door and step further into the light.*
MARYLOU *is long-bodied, dumb, sweet.* CODY *is electric, intensely alive, with an air of preoccupied frenzy — almost bursting with animal energy*)

IRWIN: My name's Irwin. Irwin Goldbook.

MARYLOU: (*Giggles again*) Everything's sure funny here.

IRWIN: (*Beaming*) You sense it immediately, eh? Ah yes
— there's much serious joy and gloom here. I myself
am a big dignified poet, with only one important
ambition in life: *to have a voice in the supermarket.*
(MARYLOU *giggles*)
No — *two* ambitions: to arrange *at once* for the publication of all my friends' writing!

CODY: You're all writer-fellas, huh?

IRWIN: We're big international traveling authors. We
sign autographs for old ladies from Ozone Park! (*To*
CODY) And you're Abner Yokum — or is it Gene Autry?

CODY: (*Laughing*) Nah, I'm just the son of an old Okie
Shadow . . .

IRWIN: (*Excited*) What, what? Another archetype? Another type for the Ark?

25

KEROUAC: *(Mock disgust at the pun)* . . . Irwin!

CODY: Yassir, born in a jalopy as my folks were makin' their way from Iowa to LA, eyes fixed anxious on the road . . . where I been ever since . . .

KEROUAC: *(Excited)* You really been around, huh? . . .

CODY: Seen it all, m'boy . . . shiny swath of headlamps shimmerin' astral-like down the road . . .

IRWIN: *(Delighted)* My God! An Ode from the Plains! A wild yea-sayer! — what a *find!* *(Hopefully)* Were your parents . . . uh . . . *real* Okies?

CODY: Nah — Pa had a barber trade — till Ma died when I was two. Then he became the most totterin' bum on Larimer Street. He and me hoboed all over the Southwest.

KEROUAC: Wow! That's what I'm gonna do!

IRWIN: You've never been to *school?* How marvelous!

CODY: Why sure I been to school! Spent *all* my time in the library — 'cept a'course for a few innings out in, how you say, the pool hall and jail. First-class altar boy, too. Priests loved me in every Catholic church in Colorado!

IRWIN: *(Overcome)* How did you *get* here?

CODY: *(Proud)* Drivin' a 'thirty-two Pontiac clunker, the Green Hornet. . . . Didn't have to steal it, neither. Marylou here turns a trick now and then.

IRWIN: You're going to *love* New York! I have to take you *at once* to the Nickel-O!

CODY: Hey, man — you think you could rustle us up a little grub? Got any eggs maybe we could fry? Ain't had a bite all day and Marylou here's about to faint on me.

MARYLOU: Am not, either.

CODY: Now, darling, here we are in New York and it is absolutely necessary to postpone all those leftover things concerning our personal lovethings . . . *(To* IRWIN*)* Did you say you had somethin' to eat?
 *(*IRWIN *jumps up and heads for the kitchen)*

IRWIN: Yes! All sorts of things! Cloverleaf jam, Swieback crackers, hundred-year-old Chinese eggs -- we'll pour all kinds of good things into you . . . *(*HE *exits)*

CODY: *(Calling after* IRWIN*)* So long's I can get this lil old girl something to *eat,* son, y'ear me? I'm *hungry,* I'm *starving,* let's *eat right now! (To* KEROUAC*)* You don't seem to say much, man. Cat got your tongue?

KEROUAC: *(Stunned)* . . . uh . . . Irwin does most of the talking . . . I'm . . . I'm not much of a talker.

CODY: Well I know what you mean, yass, absolutely . . . Marylou's a lot like that, aren't you, darlin' . . .

MARYLOU: Ah dunno . . . Ah just try to get along . . . Ah —

CODY: — 'Cause you do, darlin', now you just come over here, honeythighs, you sit next to me, 'cause now is the time and *we all know time! (*MARYLOU *moves away)* I've pleaded and pleaded with Marylou for a peaceful sweet understanding of pure love between us forever with all hassles thrown out. But her mind is bent on something else.

KEROUAC: *(Dumbfounded)* . . . uh-huh . . . yes, women aren't easy to understand . . .
 *(*MARYLOU *giggles)*

CODY: We blame on them and it's all our fault.
 *(*MARYLOU *plops down in* CODY's *lap)*

27

But peace will come suddenly, we won't understand when it does — see, man?

KEROUAC: You been to California, too?

CODY: Well a'course — sweet zigzaggin' every side . . .

KEROUAC: That's what I gotta do . . .

MARYLOU: Ah like Denver better . . .

CODY: Now darlin', it is absolutely necessary at once to begin thinking of our specific worklife plans!

IRWIN: *(Yelling in from the kitchen)* I'm heating chop suey! On its way!

CODY: Wonderful, perfect! Now dammit, look here — we all must admit that everything is fine and there's no need in the world to worry, and in fact we should realize what it would mean to us to *understand* that we're not *really* worried about *anything?* Am I right?

KEROUAC: How old are you?

CODY: Almost nineteen! Marylou here's only a child — mah child bride of fifteen.

MARYLOU: . . . told you I dint wanna get married . . . jes no point to it . . .

CODY: *(Laughing)* Oh honey Marylou, how sweet you musta been at *nine!* Think of all that time we coulda been back of the garage.

MARYLOU: Ah don't like New York . . .

CODY: When I see a sidewalk never can resist the urge to —
    (IRWIN reappears)

IRWIN: — come and get it!

CODY: Wheeoo! Here it is, darlin'! *(Stentorian)* I can't think of nothin' in my interior concerns but caterin' to the amazement and gratitude I feel for you fine people!

> (MARYLOU *and* IRWIN *exit to kitchen.* CODY *starts to follow, realizes* KEROUAC *is lingering, turns back to him, grinning)*

Why, man, we'll roll it *coast to coast!*

KEROUAC: *(Delighted, stumbling)* What . . . what's your name?

CODY: *Cody* — Cody Pomeray. Fastest man alive! Jes leapin' with lovelooks! C'mon — *let's eat!*

> *(Blackout)*

SCENE 3

Early morning. Wooded area. The outline of a battered old car is barely visible to the side. RUTH *and* MARYLOU *are curled up in sleeping bags.* CODY *and* KEROUAC, *just awake, are enjoying the sunrise, making some halfhearted efforts to clean up the campsite.*

CODY: — yup, that trail to Heaven is a long, long trail. But y'see m'boy, there's no need to worry — 'cause we're already *there!*

KEROUAC: Sure feels that way this morning. *(Looking around happily)* Never seen such beautiful country.

CODY: Lots of it — and we're gonna see it all.

KEROUAC: *(Gesturing toward* RUTH *and* MARYLOU*) If* our beauties ever wake from their Snow White sleep.

CODY: Not Snow White — Sleeping Princess. Can't you college boys keep your fairy tales straight?

KEROUAC: My crowd was into *Thrilling Detective* magazine.

CODY: Deprived mill-town youth. Y'lucky ah come along, boy, got you outta that tiny 'lil life, eh? That Lo-well Massa-*tu*-setts Saturday-night popcorn jamboree. You diggin' this sun, Jack? Damn! Bam!
(CODY *dances around maniacally*)

KEROUAC: Shush, Cody . . . you'll wake the girls.

CODY: No way, m'boy. Not after last night's workout. That is (*Laughs*), if they got as confused as *we* did! Ah swear at one point there ah had sweet *Ruthie* in mah arms, while you and Marylou were —

KEROUAC: (*Embarrassed*) — what am I gonna say to Marylou? What am I gonna say to *Ruthie?* We've never done anything like *that* before . . .

CODY: *Never* done —?! (*Heads toward the women*) Wahl, ah guess you need a little more practice then!

KEROUAC (*Grabbing* CODY) Stop! — wait! You keep this up, you're gonna turn me into a spindly 'lil Will Hubbard!

CODY: That shy lil bank clerk?

KEROUAC: Irwin thinks he's "marvelous" . . . part of the great molecular comedown . . . My pa kept warnin' me about hanging around with "nonathletic Jewish kids."

CODY: With *all* them college creep-os . . .
(THEY *break up in laughter.* RUTH *begins to stir in her sleeping bag*)

KEROUAC: Pa sure raised Hell when I wouldn't go back to Columbia — "throwin' it all away," he said, "chance to make real contacts, do something big in the world."

CODY: 'Thass jes what you're doin'! — travelin' around with me and becomin' a big artist-type writer. Right, m'boy?

KEROUAC: Pa says "No Kerouac was ever an artist . . . never was such a name in the artist game."

CODY: Wha—?! Does he want you to talk and write jes like everybody else?

KEROUAC: Cody, you understand completely.

CODY: A'course ah do. Always have. It's my amazin' intu-ee-tive power.

KEROUAC: Thing is, ya see, my folks always had it tough. Pa workin' in other men's printing shops, Ma spending most of her life in a shoe factory or as a maid in —

CODY: *(Interrupting, emphatic)* — 'cause they let the world *CATCH* 'em! The secret, m'boy, is to *keep movin'!*
(HE starts dancing around again, yelling Indian war whoops)
Like a young idjit Injun in the sagebrush! Whoo! Whoo!

RUTH: *(Sticking her head out of sleeping bag)* I thought Tonto and the Lone Ranger had gone off the air? What a sight to start the day . . .

KEROUAC: *(Starting toward RUTH, embarrassed)* Hey, Ruthie . . . uh . . . mornin', m'love . . . got some breakfast over here, if —
(CODY grabs KEROUAC and holds him back)

CODY: Well, well, beauty's on the rise! *(To KEROUAC)* Let's give these gals a proper mornin' serenade!
(HE starts singing, coaxing KEROUAC along with the words)

CODY and KEROUAC:
Oh, gimme a home
where the buffalo roam
and the deer and the —

CODY:
— not-so-dear play . . .

KEROUAC and CODY:
Where nuthin' is heard
but the sorrowin' word
and the —

(MARYLOU *slowly sticks her head out of her sleeping bag.* SHE's *naked from the waist up*)

MARYLOU: *(grumpily)* Chris'sake! . . . ain't you two got nuthin' better t'do 'cept croak away like two dumb bullfrogs? . . .

(CODY *leaps over and dives onto* MARYLOU's *sleeping bag*)

CODY: Honeythighs, I got *lots* better things to do . . . jes shove your sweet little ass right on over there and ah —

MARYLOU: *(Pushing* CODY *away)* — oh no, no you don't, no more a'*that!* Ah'm *finished* with you, hear me? *(To* RUTH, *indignant)* Why that no-good cracker *hit* me last night!

(KEROUAC *and* RUTH *react with genuine surprise,* CODY *with genuine hurt*)

KEROUAC: Cody wouldn't do a thing like —

RUTH: — of all the rotten —

CODY: — *Darlin'!* What in the name of —?! These fine people here gonna — *(*MARYLOU *starts to giggle)* — gonna think ah'm some mean 'ole Okie bum if you —

MARYLOU: — oh, *awright!* *(To* KEROUAC *and* RUTH) Ah was teasin' . . .

CODY: *(Still indignant)* That is no way, darlin', I repeat, no way to talk in front of mah newfound best buddy, nor for that matter, sweet Ruthie neither —

MARYLOU: — well you *did* hit me once.

RUTH: You did?

KEROUAC: You didn't.
(CODY *draws himself up with dignity*)

CODY: Yes. *(Pause)* Ah did. *(Pause)* One time in Denver when I looked through the mail slot and saw her ballin' that sailorboy.

MARYLOU: *(Giggling)* . . . cute little blond fella.

CODY: *Ah'm* the one got hurt! Why that girl's head's so hard, it damn near broke mah *wrist!*
(THEY *all laugh.* MARYLOU *takes out a large bottle of cold cream from inside the sleeping bag.* SHE *shoves it at* RUTH *and* KEROUAC)

MARYLOU: Not as hard as this jar ah spent the night with!

RUTH: *(Reading the jar's label)* "Lady Parker's Cold Cream" —

KEROUAC: *(Reading the label)* "Super Economy Size" —
(THEY *break up laughing*)

MARYLOU: That no good sex fiend put Lady Parker all over mah sweet little —

CODY: — honeythighs, you know you scored that jar all by yourself last week in the A&P —
(Interrupts himself)
— ooh — ooh . . . don't look now, pretties, but
(A *uniformed* STATE TROOPER *walks toward them*)
an offisah-type fella jes jumped outta the piney woods . . . shiazola! *(To* MARYLOU*)* Quick — put on the over-coat!

34

MARYLOU: It's wedged between — where's mah clothes, where's mah clothes? —

RUTH: — *under* the sleeping bag. Here, let me —
  (THEY *freeze as the* TROOPER *saunters up*)

CODY: (*Unctuous, ridiculous*) Hi there, offisah, beautiful day, eh? Sure is wonderful country you got in these parts —

TROOPER: (*Southern accent*) Mighty glad y'all like it. We're famous in Texas for our — hospitality.

CODY: Yass, exactly, thas jes what I was tellin' my friends here — in Texas, I told 'em, why people can't hardly do enough for ya, they's just about *the* most cordial, friendliest folk in all mah worldly —

KEROUAC: (*Trying to shut* CODY *up*) — didn't think they'd be any harm in our camping out for just one night, officer. That's our car right over there and we'll be heading off in less time than it —

TROOPER: (*To* MARYLOU) — If those are your clothes ah passed on mah way down here, ma'm, you best stay in that sleeping bag. You see, we got a statewide ord'nance in these friendly parts 'gainst what we call "indecent exposure" — public nudity?

MARYLOU: (*Mumbling*) He mean me? . . . (*Indignant*) Well ah never in all mah born days —

KEROUAC: (*Interrupting*) — Hush up, Marylou . . .

CODY: (*To* TROOPER, *pretending to be dumbfounded*) Bless my soul, how customs do change from place to place!

TROOPER: You folks from these parts?

MARYLOU: We're from Colorado. Them two's (*Pointing to* RUTH *and* KEROUAC) from New Yor—

CODY: *(Trying to shut her up)* — oh my, *no!* — see, we been travelin' 'round, jes goin' here and there . . . with that sun beatin' down ah said to them, "Now you all do as I'm doin', disemburden yourself of them clothes, jes open up your pretty bellies as we drive into that sun . . ."

TROOPER: Mmm . . . does get hot in these parts.
(HE reaches down and picks up the jar of cold cream)
But applyin' this to your bodies, jes gonna make you hotter — know what I mean?
(MARYLOU giggles)
Especially if these young ladies do the applyin' —

KEROUAC: That's mine, officer. I got this rash, you see, and the doctor told me —

TROOPER: — well, a'course he did. Mighty easy to get a rash travelin' round in mixed company.

CODY: — yass, well we sure do love this here Sonora county, offisah, watchin' all them ranchers lopin' up and down, every one a millionaire I betcha . . . *(Giggles maniacally)* yass, yass, if I lived round here I'd go be an idjit in the sagebrush, that right, jes an idjit in the sagebrush . . . hee-hee-hee . . .

TROOPER: *(Laconic)* I'd say you're well on your way, son.

CODY: Yass sir, offisah, thas right!

TROOPER: You folks got a destination — a place y'all plannin' to stop on your way to the sun?

CODY: Destination *MARS!* Thas' it, *MARS!*

MARYLOU: *Ma's* — mah Ma's.

RUTH: We're on our way to see her mother in Santa Fe.

TROOPER: Uh-huh. Little surprise, eh?

KEROUAC: That's right, we're heading straight outta Texas, officer, straight on out . . .

TROOPER: *(Serious, laconic)* Well . . . I'll tellya what ah think . . .
(HE slowly replaces the jar on the ground)
Ah think . . . what with these two beauties sittin' round naked, that you boys 'bout the luckiest sons of bitches ah seen in a long time. *(Tips his hat)* Now you look for the diner when you get *over the state line.* Ah reckon you can manage that before breakfast.

KEROUAC: Yes, sir . . .

TROOPER: Good day, ladies . . . *(HE exits)*
(THEY all roar with delight, then quickly start gathering up their things)

CODY: Whoo! Hot damn! It's jes like Irwin sez, see — the whole world's turnin' upside down. . . . Oh, the ramifications, the infinite ramifications — but no time now, no *time!* . . .

MARYLOU: *(Holding up the overcoat that had been covering her)* Ech — cold cream *every*where!

RUTH: Whatever will your mother say?!

(As THEY laugh and head toward the car — blackout)

SCENE 4

Several years later. Denver. CODY's *living room.*

Benny Carter music plays softly in the background.

Lights slowly up. KEROUAC *is typing.* HE *pauses periodically to puff on a joint and sip beer.*

KEROUAC: *(Reading from page in the typewriter)* Have you ever seen anyone like Cody Pomeray? If you've been a boy and played on dumps you've seen him, all crazy-full of glee-mad powers, giggling with pimply girls back of fenders and weeds till some vocational school swallows his ragged blisses. . . . I've known Cody four years now . . . we been East Coast, West Coast, most places in between, concentrated energy *goin'* somewhere, a swinging group of American boys intent on *life!* Cody's by far the greatest man I ever met . . . but he's also a devil, an old witch, thinks he can read my thoughts and interrupt them on purpose *so I'll look on the world like he does . . .*

(CODY *comes breezing into the room.* HE *stops when* HE *sees* KEROUAC *working*)

— and jealous, all over. "If's anything I can't stand," Cody says, "is people fucking when I'm not involved. That is, not only in the same room, but the same floor or house or world —"

CODY: — *TIME!!*
    (KEROUAC *jumps*)
Whatjadoin'?

KEROUAC: What the Hell does it look like?

CODY: Looks like you're gettin' stoned! *Now:* we gotta move fast! M'God, boy, I'm almost twenty-*three*. And you — *wahl!* No end to the things to be done — and Evelyn's gonna be back soon. First we gotta get in my little car, go see that sweet baby-pussy Marylou, then over to Irwin's basement, move on to —

KEROUAC: — you gotta stop seeing Marylou.

CODY: Why? 'Cause you stopped seein' Ruthie?

KEROUAC: Because Marylou's *married* to someone else now. And so are you — *to Evelyn,* remember?

CODY: Everything's sweet and fine. They talk together over the tel-e-phone 'bout the ee-normous size of mah dong.

KEROUAC: *(Flustered)* Who does?

CODY: Marylou and Evelyn, a'course. *(Suddenly distracted by the music)* Did you hear that riff? Chu Berry used to blow like that. . . . They all learned from Chu. . . . Who's that, the Hawk?

KEROUAC: Benny Carter.
    (CODY *starts peeking at the page in* KEROUAC's *typewriter*)

39

CODY: . . . yass, yass . . . everythin's workin' out jes fine . . . no hassles, no infant rise of protest . . .
(KEROUAC shields the page)

CODY: You writin' about me again?

KEROUAC: Uh-huh . . .

CODY: Tellin' the tale of my spermy disorderliness, eh? Hee, hee. . . . All you done since you got to Denver is *write*. Why you been practi-cally celi-bate, 'cept for me gettin' you and Evelyn together now and then so I could watch. You puttin' Evelyn in the book, too? Tellin' how she makes me sit up straight when I watch Gangbusters?

KEROUAC: I'm sayin' you married Frank Sinatra, gave David Rose his very first kiss, and in all probability are the uncredited composer of "Laura."
(THEY laugh)

CODY: *(Grinning)* Thas fine . . . but be sure and tell the lit'rary folk ah'm the possessor of the very biggest dork in the *en*-tire West. Except that bum I told you about who used to sleep with me and Pa in the shantytown — he'd wake up mornings and have this big-piss hard-on, you know, and I was stupefied and knocked out by the size of it, see — 'cause I was only nine, a'course, and noticin' those things . . . *(Sensing KEROUAC's unease)* C'mon! *(Pulling KEROUAC to his feet)* I'll tell you about it on the way to Irwin's, m'boy — Irwin and me are embarked on a tree-mendous season together, just like when we were in New York. We're building our re-lationship, he says, like a l-o-n-g Bach fugue, see, where all the sources move in between each other, see —

KEROUAC: — you and Irwin gonna kill yourselves with those all-night bennie sessions . . .

40

CODY: Why not man? — a'course we will if we want to. How would you know anyway, you ain't been outta the house in two weeks — all that *writin'!* Now, *c'mon!*

KEROUAC: Okay, okay . . .
(EVELYN *enters the room.* SHE's *in her late twenties, warm, full-blooded, direct*)

EVELYN: Well — both husbands! Nice.

CODY: Well, yass . . . hi, darling . . . *We're about to leave.* (*Looking at his watch*) *TIME!* You don't realize or notice — it's passin' us by this very minute! No end to the things to be done!

EVELYN: Cody, they're going to write on your grave: "He Lived, He Sweated" . . .

KEROUAC: (*Laughing*) No halfway house is Cody's house.

CODY: Got to pick up the car, pick up Irwin —

EVELYN: — pick up the laundry, pick up the groceries . . .

CODY: Ain't you got 'em?

EVELYN: No, you said you would, since I had to work today.

CODY: Darlin', you know and I know that everything is straight between us, beyond the furthest abstract definition in metaphysical terms or any terms you care to specify or sweetly impose or harken back to —
(EVELYN *throws up her hands in good-natured surrender*)

EVELYN: All right, all right! What's your schedule?

CODY: Here we go! (*Consulting his watch*) Now Evelyn — it is exactly six-fourteen; I shall be back at exactly ten-fourteen, for our hour of reverie together, real sweet

41

reverie, darlin', and then, strange as it seems but as I thor-ro-ly explained . . .

(The lights begin to dim)

EVELYN: *All right!* I'll see you two later. (SHE *exits*)

CODY: See how fine she is! C'mon, boy! Time's running, run-n-*ning!* . . .

(Blackout)

SCENE 5

Three hours later. IRWIN's *basement apartment in Denver, empty except for a burning candle, an old chair, a makeshift icon, a bed.*

As lights go up, CODY *and* KEROUAC *are entering the apartment,* CODY *still at fever pitch.* IRWIN *jumps up.*

CODY: *(In mid-conversation with* KEROUAC*)* — it all goes to develop respect for the unconscious properties of the soul —

IRWIN: — where *were* you?! You said eight o'clock —

KEROUAC: *(To* CODY*)* — that's right! Got to reinvent everything.

IRWIN: — I got so worried, I wrote *three* new poems — *bad* poems!
(CODY *throws his arm around* IRWIN)

CODY: — now, Irwin, when we reach *Saturn* — where ol' Jack here will promptly turn into a *rock!* — (CODY *and* KEROUAC *start laughing*) — dependin', a'course, on the Savior's higher grace —

43

IRWIN: — Cody, calm down!

KEROUAC: How can we calm down while inventing a whole *New Way?*

CODY: Right, m'boy!

IRWIN: How can we have our session if your soul is so agitated with excitement.

CODY: *(Sidling up to* IRWIN *like Groucho Marx)* Can you shoot pool? Can you cheat at poker?
   *(*IRWIN *starts to giggle)*

CODY: *(Following up his advantage)* You can't? You don't? Then how you gonna make a *living?* — tell me *that!*

IRWIN: *(Giving up, joining in the goof)* We'll free-lance as writers for hate mail! We'll go to Paris! We'll buy islands!

CODY: *Now* you're talkin'! Got to be hot-rock capable of everything at the same time! *(Imitating W. C. Fields)* . . . Atlantéan . . . a Roman-Aryan mixture, "Jackson mah boyyyy," athletes of Sparta plus roots in nomad mio-see-an man! . . . Got the bennies?
   *(*IRWIN *goes for Benzedrine)*

KEROUAC: Got any beer?

IRWIN: You want beer *and* benny?

KEROUAC: Dunno — sure . . .
   *(*IRWIN *goes to check for beer)*

CODY: Got to meet our Karma, our earned fate . . . Jesus knew he was assigned to die for the sake of the eternal safety of mankind —

KEROUAC: — of all sensing beings.

44

CODY: No — not flying ants. Knowing it, Jesus does it, dies on the Cross — that was his Karma as Jesus. Dig what that means.

(IRWIN comes back)

IRWIN: Yes . . . we have *some* beer.

KEROUAC: *(Enthusiastic, as he moves to chair)* Aw-right now! I'm gonna sit m'self down over here and listen to you two guys talk magical words in the air!

CODY: Beautiful, man! Jack's gonna write it all down!

IRWIN: *(Slightly annoyed)* Like always . . .

KEROUAC: *(Happily)* Yup, yup . . . just an Ambitious Paranoid . . . scribbling away to keep myself company . . .

IRWIN: Jacky, you're the Holy Fool —

KEROUAC: *(Almost yelling with glee)* Yeah! We're lookin' for derangement to bring us landward back!

CODY: C'mon Irwin, open the tubes!

IRWIN: *(Cautious)* . . . then Jack, you . . . you are staying?

KEROUAC: *(Surprised)* Huh? Sure — why not?

IRWIN: Well frankly, Jack, it . . . it might interfere with Cody and me becoming absolutely honest and complete with one another . . .

CODY: Irwin — open the goddamn tubes! What difference does it make, anyway? Jack watches me and Evelyn, too . . . matter a'fact — hee, hee — I sorta dig it when Jack watches, it's like havin' a —

KEROUAC: *(Suddenly catching on, stunned)* Wha—? I thought you guys just *talked!*

45

(IRWIN *hands some soaked cotton from the Benze-*
drine tubes to CODY)

IRWIN: We do whatever we feel like doing —

KEROUAC: Wait a *minute!* Are you trying to tell me that
you two actually —

IRWIN: — and don't start acting like some shocked bishop
from Lowell warning the boys to keep their hands
above the covers at bedtime.
(KEROUAC *turns away, shaking his head in disbelief.*
CODY *hands* KEROUAC *some of the cotton*)

CODY: You *got* to start takin' your clothes off at the orgies,
Jacky m'boy . . . got to *burn* — and *burn!* . . .

KEROUAC: Lemme be . . . just lemme be . . .

IRWIN: *(To* KEROUAC, *much softer)* Ah Jack, your big
funny mind . . .

KEROUAC: *(Also softening)* You two keep this shit up, I
may go back to Ruthie . . .

CODY: Marriage is *not* the name of your Karma, m'boy
. . . Irwin, gimme another tube . . . *c'mon!*
(IRWIN *puts his arm gently around* KEROUAC'S
shoulder. KEROUAC *wiggles loose, embarrassed, but
mollified*)

KEROUAC: . . . I can't keep up with you two . . .

IRWIN: Come sit on the bed with us.

KEROUAC: . . . no, no . . . I'll rest over here . . .
doze . . .

IRWIN: Old Romeo Sadface . . . you got the biggest soul
of all . . .

KEROUAC: . . . awright, just get on with it . . . whatever the Hell it is . . .

CODY: Yass! . . . the time has *fi-nally* come for us to get *with* it . . . I feel like I could talk all night with nothin' more'n the energy of you two Karmic princes sittin' in the Denver night . . . plus a few or four bennies, a'course! *Now:* the first thing I got to talk about tonight, since Evelyn sees me as some no-good sex fiend, and Marylou as the biggest hammer in the West, is my early sex life and early life in general . . .

(KEROUAC *takes out a notebook, occasionally scribbles in it)*

IRWIN: We can't talk exclusively about matters sexual or Jack will fall into his dumb-show-avoiding-slumber . . .

KEROUAC: *(Flaring)* Stop trying to control everything! *(Quieter)* . . . just talk . . . I'll be asleep in no time . . .

CODY: Yass . . . well . . . we'll talk about — CARS! Every time I stole a car, I'd let the clutch out too fast and snap the universal joint —

IRWIN: — that's *beautiful,* Cody, the way you put that.

CODY: — not even a dream machine, not even a 1940 Cadillac Eight banger, can you be sure you won't crack the cam, too — whoo!

IRWIN: You could become the greatest poet since Rimbaud — if you'd stop rushing out to see the midget-auto races.

KEROUAC: Slow down a little.

IRWIN: Serious talkers have no time to fool around with form.

KEROUAC: How about writers?

47

IRWIN: Great writers depend on amazement, not words. That's why you're a great writer, Jack, you're always so amazed.

CODY: — so many things to get down! Why you could teach me to write, too — whoo!

IRWIN: — no more grammatical fears, modified restraints —

CODY: — Yass! You can't make it with geometry!

IRWIN: The bennies are glowing in our hearts!

CODY: Blowin' in our bladders!
   (CODY *and* IRWIN *are now sitting on the bed facing each other*)

IRWIN: All part of the spontaneous flow! — you do remember we talked last time about the spontaneous flow?

CODY: A'course, and it started a train of my own that I had to tell you . . . when I stole that last car, the only reason I stole it was because I had to find out if *I* was traveling or just the *car* was traveling, or was it just the *wheels* were rollin', or the ball bearings ball—

IRWIN: — closer, Cody . . . I have to look directly into your eyes while hearing these sweet true heart sounds . . . *(Very serious)* My need to be loved is my last attachment to the possibility of fixed states . . . though I know all that is dynasour futile and must be left behind.

CODY: Yass, yass, absolutely . . . no such thing as dependable love, not even sex, not even CARS . . .
   (*The lights begin to dim*)

IRWIN: Closer, Cody . . . closer . . .

CODY: The thing is not to get hung up. God exists without qualms. As we roll along this way, I am positive

48

beyond doubt that everything will be taken care of for us. . . . No need to run to God, 'cause we're already there. . . .

(As the lights fade out, IRWIN *and* CODY *wrap into each other's arms. Seeing them,* KEROUAC *averts his eyes. Lights out for several beats, then slowly back up.* IRWIN *and* CODY *are sprawled on the floor.)*

IRWIN: Are you being honest — I mean honest with me to the bottom of your soul?

CODY: Why do you bring that up again?
*(*CODY *whoops)*

IRWIN: That's the one last thing I have to know.

KEROUAC: *(Quietly, from the corner)* That "one last thing," Irwin, is what you can't get . . . nobody gets that last thing.

CODY: — that crazy cat's been awake all night! What were you thinkin', Jack, I mean especially the cor-por-eal aspects of —

IRWIN: — Jack, you have to stop listening in on other people's lives!

KEROUAC: Why?

IRWIN: Because it's . . . it's *bad* for you!

KEROUAC: I just don't know what you two are trying to get at. I know it's too much for anybody.

IRWIN: No, no, no . . . negative Catholic Jesuit again. You know very well — but you don't like it.

KEROUAC: Well what *is* it you're driving at?

IRWIN: *(To* CODY*)* Tell him.

CODY: You tell 'im.

49

IRWIN: . . . conclusive coming together . . . energies meeting head-on . . .

KEROUAC: See — there's nothing to tell. . . . You're very amazing maniacs, but I'm gonna tell you somethin' — you keep this up, you'll both go crazy.

CODY: *(Smiling)* Should we let you know what happens as we go along?

KEROUAC: *(Starting to lecture)* Now listen, Cody, I —
   (A knock at the apartment door)

CODY: Oo-eee, I'll bet it's Evelyn!

IRWIN: I'll bet it's Ruthie, come to reclaim her football hero.

KEROUAC: *(Angry)* That's enough, Irwin . . .
   (CODY opens the door. EVELYN hurries in)

CODY: Now lissen darlin', before you get upset and start worrisome things about which no one has any control other than —

EVELYN: — Cody, shush. There's bad news, Jack. A telegram from your mother. Your father's ill. She wants you to come home.

KEROUAC: Pa? — my Pa? Oh Christ! — oh no! . .

CODY: Hey, ol' buddy, take it easy now — *(HE puts his arm around KEROUAC's shoulder)*
   (KEROUAC recoils violently, shoves CODY away)

KEROUAC: No — NO! Get your fucking hands off me! This is what comes of all this — see? SEE! *(HE runs out)*

CODY: *(Calling after him)* Jack! Jack, it's okay, ol' buddy . . . it's gonna be okay . . .

IRWIN: Oooh, I don't like it . . .

EVELYN: Come on, you two. We got to get him on a plane. Anybody got any money?

CODY: I'll get him there on my back . . .

(Fade-out as the three of them start to leave. Lights up on opposite side of stage)

SCENE 6

The Kerouac living room in Lowell, Massachusetts, a few days later.

The interior is spotless and comfortable but showing borderline poverty — overstuffed armchairs and sofa, ancient lampshades with tassels, etcetera. Catholic religious objects are much in evidence, including a plastic statue of Sainte Thérèse, surrounded by devotional candles.

As lights go up, EMIL KEROUAC's *loud laugh booms out.* HE's *sitting in an armchair, wrapped in blankets. In his fifties,* HE's *still powerfully built, volatile, loud — and kindhearted. Like his wife,* GABRIELLE, HE *speaks with a French-Canadian accent.*

EMIL: Sure I feel good this morning! I tellya, the crud's healin' *itself.* It can happen, you know. (HE *makes the sign of the Cross, then becomes much more subdued*) . . . it could happen . . .

KEROUAC: You look good today, Pa. You musta made a killing on the horses.

(EMIL *laughs, points energetically to some scrap paper on the table*)

EMIL: Gimme those, gimme those, Jacky!
(KEROUAC *hands the papers to* EMIL. GABRIELLE KEROUAC *enters.* SHE *is about the same age as her husband, and has the same "peasant" build. On occasion a little bleak and suspicious,* GABRIELLE *is essentially cheerful, down-to-earth, accepting.* SHE *always wears a religious medal pinned prominently to her dress*)

GABRIELLE: Eh maudit! — losing all our money, ey?

EMIL: I got these horses beat so bad, I'm gonna *buy* Hialeah!

EMIL: (*Studying the papers*) Regard! I play Happy Warrior to win, he wins! I play Pumpkin to place, he places — not wins, *places!*

GABRIELLE: (*Cheerful*) We're gonna be millionaires. Again.

KEROUAC: Canucks can always count, huh, Pa?

EMIL: Math is basic, *basic!*

GABRIELLE: (*Putting on her coat*) I'll be late to the shop . . . make him more coffee, Jacky.

EMIL: He makes mud. Can't do nuthin' — except play the Carlson all day. Chekooski — *all day* yesterday!

KEROUAC: Tchaikovsky, Pa.

EMIL: Sure — correct me again! I forgot how good you were at *that!*

GABRIELLE: Emil, Dr. Schwarz will be here at three.

EMIL: He's not drainin' me again! I'm not havin' no more needles stuck in my belly!

GABRIELLE: You know he's got to get the water out. If you'd go to the hospital it wouldn't hurt so . . .

EMIL: Who said it hurt? I don't like Jewish doctors playin' with my belly, that's all. Jewish doctor, Russian Chekooski — it's a goddamn foreign takeover!

KEROUAC: *(Annoyed)* Just 'cause they're foreigners, Pa, doesn't mean they —

GABRIELLE: *(To KEROUAC, trying to change the subject)* — Jacky! Jacky! . . . I saw all those big words you pinned up on the bedroom wall. Whoever uses such words? Emil — they all begin with "U." "U-bee-quee-tu." "U-reen."

KEROUAC: Ubiquitous. Urine.

GABRIELLE: Means what? Je suis tu dumb?

KEROUAC: *Ubiquitous* means "everywhere." *Urine* means . . . uh . . . you know, pee-pee.

GABRIELLE: *(Amazed)* Gidigne? Dingdong?

EMIL: Respect for your mother, Jacky!

KEROUAC: Not the dingdong, Pa. What comes out of the dingdong.

GABRIELLE: Ai, now I know who uses them words — that Irwin Goldbook and them other New York bums —

EMIL: — the ugliest puss I ever saw. He looks like a cockroach. A cockroach with pimples.

KEROUAC: You're as good as Milton Berle.

EMIL: Irwin's like Hugh Herbert — always thrown' up his hands, yellin' "woo! woo!"

GABRIELLE: What do those bums know how to live? All you need is good food, good beds — la tranquillité qui compte! Make yourself a *haven,* and Heaven comes after.

EMIL: *(Grim chuckle)* Sure, Heaven is great. It better be, anyway . . .
(GABRIELLE *kisses* EMIL *on the forehead)*

GABRIELLE: I'll be back at six. À six heures . . .

EMILE: Angie —?
(SHE *turns back)*

GABRIELLE: Ey? — qu'tu voule, cheri?

EMIL: Embrasse moi encore . . .
(SHE *kisses him again, holding him tight)*
(Quietly) Cette maudite vie, eh?

GABRIELLE: Oui, cheri . . . oui . . . à six . . . à six heures . . . (SHE *motions for* KEROUAC *to follow her to the door)*
(THEY *step into the corridor)*

GABRIELLE: *(Picking at a rip in* KEROUAC's *collar)* Now you're home again, I fix that, ey?

KEROUAC: Aw, Ma . . .

GABRIELLE: Ah, it's good you're back, Jacky. Maybe you come with me to Sainte Agnes, ey? — we say a novena together for Papa . . .

KEROUAC: Sure, Ma . . .

GABRIELLE: "Aw, Ma," "Sure, Ma" — I don't know why you learned English for all the talking you do! Listen, Ti Jean, you'll never be sorry if you always live a clean life, like a real French-Canadian boy, the way I brought you up . . .

KEROUAC: *(Playful)* "Aw, Ma . . . sure, Ma."
(SHE *laughs)*

GABRIELLE: Gimme a kiss, ey?
(THEY *embrace*)

GABRIELLE: And here — here's a five spot . . .
(KEROUAC *tries to push the money away, but* GA-
BRIELLE *persists until* HE *pockets it*)

KEROUAC: No, Ma. I don't need that. I'm okay . . .

GABRIELLE: Weyondonc! — five dollars ain't no silverware
china bazaar. . . . *(Turning serious)* Jacky — women
are sometimes lonely, but men — ai! — men are *always*
lonely. . . . Make peace with him, Jacky, ey? . . .
(SHE *embraces him*)

KEROUAC: I will, Ma . . . I will . . .

GABRIELLE: À ce soir, mon pousse . . .

KEROUAC: . . . à six heures . . .
(GABRIELLE *exits.* KEROUAC *turns back into the living
room*)

EMIL: *(To himself)* Ai . . . it takes too long. . . . Well,
dyin's all I got left, why rush it, ey?
(HE *winces with pain*)

KEROUAC: You okay, Pa?

EMIL: Ai mauva —!

KEROUAC: What is it, Pa, what's causin' the pain?

EMIL: The philosopher wants to know what causes pain,
ey? If you hadn't quit Columbia, you'd have the
answers to those questions. (HE *winces again*) Ai! . . .
birth causes all pain, sonny, that's what — *birth!* That's
why we're born, so there can be dyin'. Put that in your
book, sonny . . . *(Subsides)* . . . ah, better . . . it's
better . . .

KEROUAC: I'll make coffee for you.

EMIL: I don't want no coffee. It makes water . . . It's awright — I'm awright now. . . . Ça s'en vas, it's everyone's lot . . .

(Pause)

KEROUAC: Does Ma always leave so early?

EMIL: That poor girl — works in the shoeshop all day while I sit here figuring the horses . . . in the hospital they got no radio, you can't figure the horses, you just lie there doin' nuthin' . . .

(HE slaps the armchair with frustration)

. . . if I had done the right thing! . . . so many things I could've done! *(Tearful)* Oh God, how short it all is — just a snap of the fingers. . . . I want to be in the *middle* of life . . .

KEROUAC: *(Mournful, embarrassed)* Aw Pa . . . please, Pa . . .

EMIL: *(Violent)* Whatsa matter? — I can't cry? — 'cause I'm not some fancy Russian composer, some Chekooski? You told me he'd just throw himself on the bed sometimes and cry — "wonderful!" you said, "wonderful!" Hah! — it means a hell of a lot when *they* cry . . . 'cause he's a famous man and they all write about him. . . .

KEROUAC: C'mon, Pa! — I never said that!

EMIL: Ah, you damn kids — you think you can do what you want *all* your life! . . . *(Sadly)* It's a beautiful dream you have when you're young, before you learn how men — how things — can break . . . Jacky, it's *hard* to make a living!

KEROUAC: *(Quietly)* I don't want a living. I want life.

EMIL: You're just playing with words, sonny — words you learned in books . . . *(Weakening)* . . . I had all the time, all the time — and no more . . . ah, what a chunky little kid you were . . . strong as an ox . . . and smiling, always smiling . . . *(Starts to doze off)*

KEROUAC: *(Choked up)* . . . I'm — I'm still smiling, Pa . . .

EMIL: . . . that's right, my poor little boy . . . that's how I want your life . . . to . . . be. . . . Ti Mon Pousse . . . *(His head drops. KEROUAC doesn't see.)*
(KEROUAC paces, then turns to face EMIL)

KEROUAC: Hey, Pa . . . look, I wanna tellya that . . . I mean, Pa, why can't we . . . Oh Pa, *listen* to me!
(KEROUAC grabs EMIL's arm, suddenly realizes HE's dead)

KEROUAC: Pa! . . . Pa! . . . *(Yelling at the walls)* . . . Somebody — hurry up! My father's dead! My father! What was his sin? *WHAT WAS HIS SIN?* Oh God — Somebody help me — *PLEASE!*

(Blackout)

SCENE 7

Gas station washroom on the road to Mexico City.
CODY *and* KEROUAC *are pissing in adjacent urinals.*
KEROUAC'*s mood is sullen.*

CODY: — nothin' like being back on the road, huh, m'boy? Why we could go right on to South America! Think of it — where the Injuns are seven feet tall and eat cocaine on the mountainside!

KEROUAC: Worldwide band of wild fellahin beggars . . .

CODY: And all in this sun! Are you diggin' this Mexican sun, Jack? It makes you high — Whoo! I want to go on and on — this road drives *me!*

KEROUAC: How far to Hubbard's do you think?

CODY: Ah well, *(Laughs, W. C. Fields accent)* now you're askin' me impon-de-rables — ahem! . . . we'll be kiss-in' señoritas b'dawn! . . .

KEROUAC: Hope Irwin and Raph got to Will's okay. They should be there ahead of us.

CODY: Don't know why Irwin took that bus. Gettin' awful cautious, yass, cautious. *(Laughing)* He's gettin' too many poems published, you all are, makes you cautious and calculatin'.

KEROUAC: Makes you crazier. *(Pause)* Hope Irwin brings the reviews — hope the book *got* reviewed.

CODY: Relax, relax! You got it published, dintya? Wanna be like queer old Proust hisself, writin' eighty-seven volumes? Relax!

(CODY finishes, starts washing his hands at the sink)

KEROUAC: Hey, Cody — dig this trick! *(KEROUAC stops pissing, moves to the next urinal and starts to piss again)*

CODY: Yes, man, that's a very good trick . . . but awful on your kidneys . . . awful kidney miseries for the days when you sit alone on park benches . . .

KEROUAC: I'm no old fag, you got to warn me about my kidneys.

CODY: *(Amazed)* No old —? Whoa, m'boy!

KEROUAC: ". . . queer old Proust hisself . . ."

CODY: Why man, a no-account little joke that —

KEROUAC: — I don't want to hear any more about it.

CODY: *(Hurt)* . . . well, how about that . . . *(Sad)* here we been havin' this real going goofbang together, no hassles . . . I'm surprised at you, Jack . . .

(CODY kicks open washroom door, walks out into sun. KEROUAC follows, somewhat repentant)

KEROUAC: You gotta stop thinking up new gags about my kidneys . . .

CODY: . . . oh man . . .

KEROUAC: You take more bennies than I do! I can't help it if my legs start to swell. . . . You shouldn't make fun of your friends . . .
(CODY *shakes his head sadly*)

CODY: . . . No man, no man, you got it all wrong, completely wrong . . . now you got me cryin' . . .

KEROUAC: Ah hell, you never cry. You don't die enough to cry.

CODY: You say that? . . . No man, I was cryin' . . .

KEROUAC: Come on — you're just mad . . .

CODY: Believe me, Jack, really do believe me if you've ever . . . *(Trails off)*

KEROUAC: *(Subdued)* Ah, shit, Cody . . . I don't know how to be close to — I don't know what to do with these — things. I hold them in my hand like . . . like pieces of crap and don't know where to put 'em down . . . not even *my father, my father,* when he . . .

CODY: . . . yes man, yes man . . .

KEROUAC: It's not my fault. . . . Nothin' in this lousy world is my fault!

CODY: . . . please harken back and believe me . . .

KEROUAC: I do believe you, I do . . .

CODY: No pitch, man, I only want you to know what's happenin', I —

KEROUAC: — I *do* believe you, man . . .
(*Pause*)

CODY: Now hold out your hand . . .

KEROUAC: Huh?

61

CODY: C'mon, c'mon!

>   (KEROUAC *opens the palm of his hand.* CODY *places a crystal in it*)

CODY: That's for you, Jack. Traded my wristwatch for it!

KEROUAC: *(Touched, embarrassed)* Aw, Cody, I can't —

CODY: — Shush! It's the wildest, strangest of all the crystals, probably the soul of the big chief himself. Traded for it with that little Indian girl come up to me on that mountain road while you were relievin' your, ah — kidneys — ahem!

KEROUAC: *(Looking at the crystal)* . . . it's a beautiful thing, Cody . . .

CODY: A'course it is! And that dear child picked it from the mountain jes for us. . . . Ah, Jack, she broke mah heart, murmurin' all those loyalties and wonders . . .

>   (HE *closes* KEROUAC's *palm over the crystal*)

And now the big chief hisself has got it back again . . . yass, yass, it's all workin' out jes the way it should. . . .

KEROUAC: *(Near tears)* I'll cherish it . . . cherish it all my years . . .

CODY: Now, Jack, we're goin' to leave behind us here this little trouble we had . . . just go ahead with our faces stuck out like *this*, you see, and *understand* the world as others haven't done before us. . . . *(Peering into the distance)* . . . think of this big continent ahead of us, and those Sierra Madre mountains we saw in the movies, jungles all the way down . . .

KEROUAC: Right, old buddy . . . why we're on the same route of old American outlaws skippin' the border to Monterrey. . . . Picture that grayin' desert, Cody, the ghost of an old Tombstone hellcat making his lonely gallop into the unknown . . .

CODY: *(Smiling)* Now you're seein' further again — it's the world! Now *c'mon* — we gotta find the local whorehouse, or I'll be whacking off all the way to Hubbard's. *Let's move!*

(Blackout)

SCENE 8

Lights up on split set: WILL HUBBARD's *living quarters and its backyard, outside Mexico City. Dusk.* CODY *is asleep on the ground.* KEROUAC *and a Mexican woman,* TRISTESSA, *are curled up together.*

Loud police whistles from offstage.

KEROUAC: *(Alarmed)* Huh? — who's there?

CODY: What? What? . . . Where?
    (Voice from behind tree; fake Spanish accent)

VOICE *(Irwin):* Geev up, Americanos! Geev up! Es polícia, polícia!

VOICE *(Raphael):* You — are — surrounded!
    (IRWIN and RAPHAEL come out from behind trees)

IRWIN: We have come to get you crazee Amer-ee-can poets!

CODY: . . . Irwin! . . . Whoopee!
    (EVERYONE lets out whoops of delight and greetings. CODY and IRWIN embrace)

64

KEROUAC: Whereya *been?* You're three days late!

IRWIN: Such adventures! We spent a day with — William Carlos Williams!

RAPHAEL: We read him all our stuff — and yours —

IRWIN: — and he listened and listened, and then he said "Keep on writing like that!" So you see, it's happenin', Jack, it's *happenin'!*

RAPHAEL: He's the only poet *old* enough to understand us!
   (THEY *all laugh in appreciation)*

IRWIN: Raphael's been writing big mad poems all the way down from Tijuana about the doom of Mexico . . .

RAPHAEL: I don't *like* it here — There's *death* in Mexico —

CODY: It's hotter here than a Denver pool hall, but the girls! — ah, Raph . . . wait'll we tellya about the whorehouse in Gregoria.

TRISTESSA: *(Frightened, to* KEROUAC*)* Who theese men? Crazy men, no?

KEROUAC: . . . my brothers . . .

TRISTESSA: . . . brothers? . . .

IRWIN: . . . just what I like to see, boys and girls — and boys — all curled up together!

RAPHAEL: Who's the gorgeous doll?

KEROUAC: *(To* TRISTESSA*)* . . . Si, si, new kind of brothers . . . Irwin, Raph — this is Tristessa — she's a friend of Will's —

CODY: Jack got so drunk in the whorehouse in Gregoria, he ended up with a huge broad from Venezuela — and a dog that bit his leg —!
(THEY *all laugh*)

IRWIN: Where *is* Will?

RAPHAEL: (*Looking at* TRISTESSA) Ah, Jack, you have all the luck.
(HUBBARD *enters the yard from the living quarters*)

KEROUAC: Will's taking a nap.

HUBBARD: (*Sleepily*) Not any longer. Such carnivorous shouting . . . I knew it had to be you . . .

IRWIN: Will! — We're here, we're here!
(IRWIN *embraces* HUBBARD, *who's pleased but holds to his mocking posture*)

HUBBARD: Welcome, welcome . . .

RAPHAEL: Why is it so hot?

HUBBARD: This is the cool season, Raphael. You'll adjust in a year or two . . .

IRWIN: We want to see Thieves' Market, Will, then Mexico City University, then —

HUBBARD: — Good heavens, why? Haven't you seen enough heart-shaped stadiums back home?

KEROUAC: (*Shy*) Hey, Irwin, did you bring, uh, any of the reviews? . . .

IRWIN: Oh Lord, yes! — I almost forgot!
(HE *rummages in his duffle bag*)

HUBBARD: Ignore reviews, Jack. They ruin concentration.

IRWIN: Here — the *Times*, THE *TIMES!* (*Reading*) ". . . in sum" — that's all I can read now, Jacky, or

Will might go back to sleep — "Jack Kerouac's *The Town and the City* is a rough diamond of a book . . . not at all an unpromising performance for a first novel. . . ."

(KEROUAC *lets out a low whistle of pleasure, takes the review from* IRWIN *and starts reading it to himself*)

IRWIN: Of course, they don't understand the book! It's not a novel, it's a big hymn, an epic poem!

HUBBARD: Stop inciting Jack. Sounds like a quite decent review for a first book. Anything *more* favorable and Jack would go on writing in the same style.

KEROUAC: *(Exuberant)* By the time I'm done, I'll write down everything that ever happened on the earth *in detail!*

HUBBARD: That's still Thomas Wolfe, pseudo-lyrical insatiability. Don't bore me with your New England dreams . . .

CODY: Yeah — borin' —

IRWIN: Never mind! You'll be dancing naked on your fan mail in no time! Big Faulkners and Hemingways will grow thoughtful thinking of you!

HUBBARD: Irwin: stop sounding Orphic.

IRWIN: *You* got me interested in Orphism.

RAPHAEL: When I peed in my sheets as a kid, I knew it was all gonna be creepy.

KEROUAC: Without you, Irwin, I wouldn't have got this one published.

IRWIN: I hereby predict the new one will be out *within* a year! Even idiot publishers will see at first look that "On the Road" is big mad book to change America!

RAPHAEL: "On the Road"? Is that the title? Sounds like a Dorothy Lamour movie.

HUBBARD: Why does Raphael always yell?

IRWIN: That's the way he talks. It's just as good as silence.

RAPHAEL: Good as gold.

CODY: *(Angry)* You wanna know the first sentence of *my* book? — *I take my friends too seriously!* That's the first sentence of *my* book!

KEROUAC: . . . great . . . what's the second sentence?

CODY: *Either that or I don't like life anymore.*

RAPHAEL: Next sentence: *Church music, that's best, just like Artie Shaw said.*

HUBBARD: A little codeine cough syrup, anyone?

CODY: *(Quieter, to* KEROUAC*)* "On the Road" is the one about you and me, right?

KEROUAC: *(Embarrassed)* Yeah, sorta . . . our adventures and your . . . rhythm . . .

IRWIN: *Into* the experience, not around it.

CODY: . . . runnin' up and down the changes — like how we *live!*

HUBBARD: *(Dry)* It's not how *I* live.

IRWIN: It's time for the *poets* to influence American civilization!

HUBBARD: *(Laconic)* If you'd seen a vision of eternity, Irwin, you wouldn't care about "influencing American civilization." Now sit down . . .

IRWIN: *(Respectful)* Have you been writing, Will?

HUBBARD: I have limited energy. I write *or* talk.

IRWIN: Don't be mean, Will. . . . Look, we're all here together again . . .

HUBBARD: "Together"! Like that Cupid's arrow you drew for me with our two hearts "together"? — except the arrow went through *one* heart! That's it, that's just what I mean.

IRWIN: *What,* Will?

HUBBARD: Autocratic people can only fall in love with themselves.

KEROUAC: Or the image of what they'd like to be . . .

IRWIN: *(Hurt)* That's not fair, Will . . .

KEROUAC: . . . I've been tryin' to write about that . . .

HUBBARD: Some people get high on drugs, others on introspection.

RAPHAEL: *(Yelling) Hubbard!* — I'm sick and tired of all you literary fuck-ups! I wanna meet counts and prince*sas*! I want velvet drapes, a velvet hood on my Leonardo head! I want Shelley and Chatterton in my chair. I want —

HUBBARD: *(Dry)* — oh my, so many *wants* . . . *I* want morphine . . .
(TRISTESSA *reacts to the word*)

TRISTESSA: Morphina?

HUBBARD: Si, si . . . *(Beaming)* Mexico has *wonderful* doctors . . .
(TRISTESSA *and* HUBBARD *exit to the living quarters, start boiling down morphine tablets in spoons. It's now almost dark in the yard*)

RAPHAEL: *(To* KEROUAC*)* You and Irwin are off eating international roast beefs — me, I'm suppose'ta stick to great horror poems on gutters and tenements!

(HUBBARD *and* TRISTESSA *bend over cotton, hypodermics, etcetera, with absorption)*

CODY:*(Calling out)* Think I'll join your crowd, Will. *(Almost to himself)* All these urgencies anxious and whiney.

KEROUAC: You talkin' to me, Cody?

CODY: *(Angry)* Now man, that's profoondified.

KEROUAC: *(Bewildered)* Huh?

RAPHAEL: *(To* KEROUAC *and* IRWIN*)* You both think you know everything, you think you're the only ones!

IRWIN: You, *too,* Raph — we're originating a whole new way, innocent go-ahead confession, no redoing, no —

RAPHAEL: — don't gimme that "spontaneous" bullshit! You write too fast! You need *craft!*

> HUBBARD: *(To* TRISTESSA*)*
> Looks like pretty good
> stuff.

KEROUAC: Craft is crafty.

CODY: *(Yelling out to* HUBBARD*)* Hey, Will — you got an ice-cream soda? *(Almost to himself)* What am I doin' down here?

IRWIN: *(Startled, goes over to* CODY*)* To be with me of course.

CODY: Well and yes, of course, wanted to see you — glad of you — love you as ever . . .

IRWIN: We're going to work on regularizing your energy. You have to learn to control those forces in you.

CODY: Thas jes what Evelyn says when *she* wants somethin' outta me.

HUBBARD *(To TRISTESSA, feeling the veins on his arm)* . . . no, it's raw. I'll have to try the leg again . . . *(HE searches for a spot on his thigh, then sinks the needle in)*

IRWIN: *(Hurt)* It's for our ongoing opening-up.

CODY: *(Cynical)* So we can be straight in our souls. . . . Right, Jack?

KEROUAC: *(Distracted, reading review)* Huh? . . . oh sure, ol' buddy . . .

CODY: Yass, sure, ol' buddy . . . everybody openin' up — to wraparound words! The *pull* of that lit'rary Mars, man . . .

(KEROUAC looks up and sees CODY and IRWIN standing close to each other)

KEROUAC: Hey, you two . . . don't start that "sweet-true-heart-sounds" shit again . . .

(HUBBARD and TRISTESSA return to the yard. Both lie down)

CODY: *(Angry)* What the Hell difference does it make to you? I do what I wanna do. . . . You and your reviews! *You* got no life except as a writer. You'll be an empty orphan sitting nowhere, sick and alone . . . betta be careful, Jack . . .

KEROUAC: *You* betta be careful, too.

HUBBARD: *(Almost inaudible)* . . . mmm . . . we must all be more careful . . .

71

CODY: Ah'm gettin' mighty sick a' all you preacher boys . . . *(To* KEROUAC*)* Loosen up, man — and *lay off!*

KEROUAC: I'm warnin' you, that's all . . .

CODY: Nobody *warns* me, m'boy. Ah live m'own life. That's *it* for Cody! *(*HE *starts to leave.* IRWIN *runs frantically after him)*

IRWIN: Cody, what's the matter? — wait! . . . there are lots of good things ahead . . .

CODY: Not for me. I'm splittin'. Right now *(*HE *exits)*

IRWIN: *(Following* CODY *offstage)* Wait! . . . oh please wait! . . .

RAPHAEL: Looks like the cowboy's off to a new frontier. *(Yelling)* Hey, Irwin — I keep tellin' ya — ya can't get everyone in the same bathtub together! *(*HE *laughs, slumps in hammock, nods off)*

HUBBARD: *(Mumbling)* . . . Irwin always did overestimate the charm of . . . being human . . . *(*HE *passes out.* CODY *returns with a satchel,* IRWIN *hanging on his arm)*

IRWIN: . . . it'll all work out . . . you'll see . . . we'll work it out! *(*CODY *throws off* IRWIN'*s arm, starts to leave)*

KEROUAC: Cody — hey! . . . wait a minute . . .

CODY: No way, man. I'm catchin' a freight tonight . . . going back to Evelyn, straight on through . . .

KEROUAC: . . . all that again?

CODY: . . . goin' back to mah life . . . *(*HE *turns to leave)*

KEROUAC: Why? . . . why ya goin'?

CODY: I come, I'm gone. . . . Cody's tired of cultured tones, dainty explicity. . . . Nuthin' more for me here. *(Directly to* KEROUAC) You got my rhythm — that's all you want, right?

KEROUAC: *(Upset)* . . . sorry you had to make the trip . . .

CODY: Wahl, can't talk it no more . . . makin' logic when there's only sorrowful sweats. . . . Don't kick around the gong too much, fellas. . . .
(HE turns to face KEROUAC. *Deeply felt)*
Old fever Jack . . . good-bye . . .
(HE exits. IRWIN *goes wailing after him, but stops at the edge of yard)*

IRWIN: . . . Cody . . . *Cody!* . . . *(Pause)* Please . . . get back . . . safe . . .
(IRWIN sinks to the ground, crying)
Oh God . . . my heart's broken . . .

KEROUAC: . . . 'tsall settled . . . all settled . . .

IRWIN: . . . *why?* . . . why did he go?
(KEROUAC grabs a bottle and starts to chug-a-lug it)

KEROUAC: We should all go home . . . lie down . . . rest . . . *("Laughs")* I wanna eat Wheaties by my Ma's kitchen window. . . . Ooh, I feel like a giant cloud leanin' on its side . . . *(Singing)* "It's the turn of the century, it's the turn of the century . . ."

IRWIN: *(Tearful)* . . . I wish I was a giant cloud . . .

KEROUAC: *(Drunken)* "Girls are pretty
But their cherries are itty
And if they ain't got cherries . . ."
(HE kneels down and shakes TRISTESSA)
S'funny, I'm so horny. . . . Hey, Tristessa? . . . Tristessa?
(SHE moves and groans)

KEROUAC: Hey, babe, you and me . . .

TRISTESSA: *(Barely audible)* . . . mmm . . . si . . . dor-
miendo . . .

KEROUAC: Ah, Tristessa, you're like a madonna . . .
generous and good . . .

TRISTESSA: . . . faltas . . . muchas faltas . . .

KEROUAC: A madonna of suffering. . . . Hey, Irwin,
what's gonna become of us, huh? . . . where we all
gonna be in twenty years?

IRWIN: . . . it would have worked out . . . we could
have worked it out . . .

KEROUAC: Whaddaya talkin' about now?

IRWIN: Oh, Jack — you know Cody and I were lovers!
. . . don't be an ostrich.

KEROUAC: Sure, sure . . . that's why he fucked half the
whorehouse in Gregoria.
   (KEROUAC nudges TRISTESSA harder)
You think it would be wrong if I took her while she
was out cold?

IRWIN: Yes.

KEROUAC: Mmm. . . . So do I . . .

IRWIN: I wanted classical angels . . . hand in hand . . .

KEROUAC: *(Flaring)* You *still* on that shit?! Raph's right
— you're all crazy! You love Cody, Hubbard loves you,
Cody loves . . . Cody loves . . . ? I'm tired of all this
love shit between grown-up men . . .

IRWIN: Love is love. . . . You went to church too much.

KEROUAC: Irwin, *shut up!* . . . it's unnatural . . .

IRWIN: *Not* being able to love, *yes.* . . . Who do you
love, Jack?

74

KEROUAC: Listen, little Irwin, don't think you can say *any*thing to me —

IRWIN: Can't I?

KEROUAC: *Love* — big bullshit word! You mean whose slit do I wanna eat? Whose cunt do I wanna hammer? Just 'cause you're a smart-assed little Jewish queer — you and your aching fairy woes —

IRWIN: — you and your lumberjack tears . . . buried and bereft American man . . .

KEROUAC: *(Angry)* I'm gonna stick it to her!

IRWIN: No, you're not. . . . *That's* unnatural.

KEROUAC: Oh yeah? — (HE *wheels around)* — then stick it in your face!
    (Pause)

IRWIN: *(Quietly, firmly)* Jack . . . I'll blow you . . . I love you, Jack . . .
    (KEROUAC *hesitates a beat, then walks toward* IRWIN)

KEROUAC: *(Softly)* . . . what the hell . . . you always had a big mouth . . .

    (Blackout)

Act Two

SCENE 1

A shabby apartment in Richmond Hill, 1955. The same religious objects are visible as in act one, scene 6 (for example, the statue of Sainte Thérèse). KEROUAC is alone, seated cross-legged in the middle of the room, meditating. HE is shabbily dressed and has aged noticeably — hair receding, the beginning of a paunch, et cetera. Periodically, he winces with pain, pulls up a trouser to rub his leg for relief — revealing that the leg is bandaged.

GABRIELLE enters the apartment carrying a cake box. Seeing KEROUAC cross-legged on the floor, she frowns, then slams the door with extra force. KEROUAC jumps.

KEROUAC: — Wha—? . . . Oh, mémère . . . the factory close early?

GABRIELLE: *(Angry)* Early? — it's six-thirty! You're in a trance again . . .

KEROUAC: It helps the phlebitis, Ma . . . my brain discharging the Holy Fluid . . .

   (SHE *bangs down the cake box*)

GABRIELLE: *Holy?* — envi d'chien en culotte! *(Softening)* For dessert — cakes from Cushman's . . . try the white one, vanilla . . .

    (SHE sinks into a chair, exhausted)

Ai — cette maudite vie! . . . What's gonna happen? . . .

KEROUAC: Nobody knows . . .

    (HE suddenly winces with pain)

GABRIELLE: *My* legs have to pain — standing ten hours! Yours you *make* pain! . . . un vrai Kerouac . . .

    (KEROUAC uncrosses his legs and gets up)

KEROUAC: It's good for me, Ma . . . holds my body to a dead stop . . . not even the shred of an "I-hope" or a Loony Balloon . . .

GABRIELLE: So who wants to get rid of hope? Whadda you, an old man? Thirty years old and he's —

KEROUAC: — thirty-three —

GABRIELLE: — bon!— thirty-three! . . . and you gotta stop hoping?

KEROUAC: Pa said life is what you smell in the Bellevue Morgue. Detachment's the one salvation, to go apart and —

GABRIELLE: *Jesus* is salvation! I brought you up to know right from wrong and what God wants of you. Écoute, Jean! —

KEROUAC: — it's awright, Ma, Jesus and Buddha are tellin' us the same thing.

GABRIELLE: Then why don't you stick to the religion you were born with, why should you need another religion?

KEROUAC: They both teach life's an illusion — empty arrangements of things that seem solid.

GABRIELLE: *(Agitated)* Whaddaya mean, empty?
(SHE *grabs her pocketbook)*
This is a pocketbook, ain't it? I'm *holdin'* it! And it ain't empty. *(Drops it in disgust)* Aw-'shu *(Starts toward kitchen)*

KEROUAC: Dinner's ready . . . I heated up the fricassee.

GABRIELLE: You shouldn't have to do that.

KEROUAC: Makes me feel good to do *somethin'* around here. You shouldn't have to work in the shoe factory.

GABRIELLE: Tiens! I did it before, I do it again . . . Besides, I like to be with people. We got alot to say. *You* don't go out enough. I think you need a new girl friend.

KEROUAC: They all look like airline hostesses, with mock teeth. Besides, the ones I go for don't go for me.

GABRIELLE: Because you never *stay* . . . always running home to keep me company.

KEROUAC: You're the woman that wants me most, Ma.

GABRIELLE: I don't need so much company. Sainte Thérèse, c'est beaucoup . . . *(Pause)* Did you write today?

KEROUAC: Sure . . . like always.

GABRIELLE: *(Teasing)* More dirty stuff you won't let your old lady read, eh?

KEROUAC: The only one I said you can't read is "The Subterraneans." You'd get mad at me.

GABRIELLE: I know — the Negro girl. Ai! I wouldn't read it anyway.

KEROUAC: *(Moody)* It would be nice to have *somebody* reading them. . . . Eleven books since *Town and the*

81

City . . . eleven books . . . and not one published . . . Crowley thinks maybe one more revision of "On the Road" and Viking might take it. . . .

GABRIELLE: They been sayin' that for five years. . . . Try not to think about it . . . it makes you drink . . . we make out, don't worry . . .
  (Pause)

KEROUAC: *(Cautious)* Got another letter from Irwin today . . . says California's fulla good young writers . . . whole new scene out there . . .

GABRIELLE: You're the best, you're here.

KEROUAC: No, no, Irwin says Japhy Ryder's the best, the best young poet in California. Japhy Ryder. Only twenty-three . . .

GABRIELLE: Such names, such people . . .

KEROUAC: *(Smiling)* Japhy told Irwin I'm a great Bodhisattva.

GABRIELLE: Great what?

KEROUAC: Great wise being . . . great wise angel . . .

GABRIELLE: Buddhists got angels, too? You're too old to be an angel.

KEROUAC: Aw Ma, ain't it the truth! . . . *(Sad)* Twenty-three . . . huh . . .

GABRIELLE: All Budd-has, with no hope, ey? Sounds like that crazy Cody.

KEROUAC: No, Cody doesn't hang out much with the new crowd . . . they say he's into Edgar Cayce . . .

GABRIELLE: Cody ye plein d'marde!

KEROUAC: Ma! — what language for a Catholic lady!
  (GABRIELLE *crosses herself*)

82

GABRIELLE: Forgive me, Sainte Thérèse. But believe me, he's worse than that.

KEROUAC: Cody's workin' hard on the railroad, buyin' things for Evelyn and the kiddies.

GABRIELLE: *(Impressed)* Eh? Good for Cody! Maybe he's not so crazy . . .

KEROUAC: *(Sad)* Wonder how he is . . . haven't heard from him in *(Figuring in his head)* — huh! years . . . *(Almost to himself)* I should be out there, see what's goin' on . . .

GABRIELLE: Ey, Jean . . . why not? *(Pause.* GABRIELLE *touches* KEROUAC *gently)* Jean?

KEROUAC: Huh?

GABRIELLE: Why not California? I need a rest from "Holy Fluids" and Buddhas . . .

KEROUAC: Would you really be okay? . . . I mean, if I went for just a little while?

GABRIELLE: Whaddayou? — some big-time entertainer? All I hear is junk about empty pocketbooks!
    *(*THEY *laugh)*

KEROUAC: You'll miss me, you'll see . . .

GABRIELLE: 'Shu! The Neigre ladies in the shoeshop make more sense.

KEROUAC: I could carry everything I need, Ma, right on my back! A regular kitchen and bedroom . . .

GABRIELLE: *(Smiling)* Don't worry. *(*SHE *pats her belly)* I got a little saved. In the corset, like always!

KEROUAC: Aw, Ma! . . . it won't cost much to hitchhike, and *(Quieter)* . . . and when I get there, maybe . . . maybe I could stay with Cody and Evelyn . . .

(HE *pours himself more liquor.* GABRIELLE *heads toward the kitchen)*

GABRIELLE: Vas, Jean, Vas! . . . Enough books! — ferme le livre — vas! But don't forget Jesus, ey? ((SHE *exits*)

KEROUAC: *(Calling after her)* I'll pray all the time, Ma, pray for all living creatures . . . *(To himself)* only decent activity left . . . just rest and be kind . . .

GABRIELLE: *(Calling out from kitchen)* You want milk, Jean?

KEROUAC: Sure — du la chocolat! . . . My stuff'll get published some day, Ma . . . then I'll buy you lots of good things!
  (GABRIELLE reenters)

GABRIELLE: Mmm . . . a lil home of my own again. *(Catching herself)* But who cares! Remember my motto: "Be glad for little favors, suspicious of big ones."

KEROUAC: *(Laughing)* I know, I know — "Hurt no one, mind your business, make a new compact with God."

GABRIELLE: *(Exiting again to kitchen)* Go tell it to those bums in California!
  (As the lights fade to out, KEROUAC raises bottle in a toast)

KEROUAC: To mémère, who's already entered perfect sainthood — and the proof is, she doesn't know it!

  (Blackout)

SCENE 2

Stage dark.

IRWIN *(Reciting; voice-over):* . . . what angry horde shadows your doorways, crumbled, disheartened, its features erased —?
Wailing of Children!
Wailing of Mothers!
Wailing of all the blue-suited men!
Wailing, America, flung in your doorways,
Wailing in tenement prisons of Grace.
Jailhouse of nations, sorrowing freedoms,
Lost in the maelstrom,
Lost in the last ship,
Lost on the voyage, last of our journey,
Lost, O America, maker of Men!

(Applause, noisy enthusiasm, over, then lights up inside JAPHY RYDER's *shack in San Francisco. People are crowding around* IRWIN, *congratulating him. The shack is bare, neat, mostly straw mats and pillows, plus a few Japanese scrolls on the walls, and piles of books. Cal Tjader records are playing softly in the background.* KEROUAC, *looking forlorn and bewildered, is wandering around)*

KEROUAC: For the wine, folks . . . help with a contribution for the wine, people . . . gotta kick in a little somethin' for the wine, everybody . . .
*(*IRWIN *and* SIMON — *young, good-looking, "dippy" — settle down together on the floor.* CACOETHES — *fat, middle-aged, self-important — is holding forth in one corner. A beautiful young woman,* PRINCESS, *is doing yoga exercises. A few people are sprawled on the floor; others drag sleeping bags and blankets out into the yard)*

SIMON: *(To* IRWIN*)* I took a raspberry pill . . .

IRWIN: Raspberry?

SIMON: Dextidrene — in my stomach . . . *(Patting it)* See? — high in my stomach I came upon Dostoevsky's *Dream of a Queer Fellow* —

IRWIN: *Dream of a Ridiculous Man*, you mean?

SIMON: . . . the possibility of love within the chasel halls of my heart . . . trees are waving at me and bowing hello.

IRWIN: Ah, dearest, you're the guard at the gate of Heaven!

SIMON: I wanna let *everyone* in!
*(*THEY *laugh and embrace.* KEROUAC, *drinking stead-*

ily, has wandered upstage and started arguing with CACOETHES *and his group)*

CACOETHES: *(Pontificating)* — no! no! The *only* important scene now is here in San Francisco. . . . Irwin's reading tonight was the first explosion, only the beginning . . .

KEROUAC: *(Sarcastic)* Irwin's from New York.

CACOETHES: The poem will make Irwin famous from coast to coast. He wails beautifully. . . . A pity we're going to lose Japhy to Japan . . . but he'll be back . . .

KEROUAC: If he's smart, he'll disappear into Central Asia with a string of yaks, selling popcorn and safety pins.

CACOETHES: *(Mocking)* Ah yes, we've heard you're "into" Buddhism. . . . Japhy thinks well of your Hanayana sutra translations. Hanayana Buddhism isn't a bad place to start, though a little dreamy. Japhy will help you move on to the Lankavatara Scriptures — though of course for *that* — for *Zen* — you'll have to learn at least *one* Oriental language.
(JAPHY — young, intense, direct — enters, hears the two arguing)

KEROUAC: I'll leave the indoorsy abstractions to you, Cacoethes. Goes with your dainty poems.
(JAPHY leaps into the air, lands near KEROUAC)

JAPHY: *(Roaring)* Yaaaaah! How ya doin', old Bodhisattva?

KEROUAC: Hey — Japhy! You're just in time — Cacoethes is gonna recite his *grrreat* poems for us. *(Mimicking)* "The duodenal abyss that brings me to the margin consuming my flesh . . ."

87

CACOETHES: Bravo! Bravo! Now you must recite one of yours, one of those earthy epics about freight trains and the *wonder* of exchanging butts with bums.

(JAPHY pulls KEROUAC away)

JAPHY: *(Over his shoulder to CACOETHES, good-natured)* You old fart! . . . C'mon, Jack . . .

KEROUAC: *(Yelling over to CACOETHES)* . . . bunch of *athletes* . . . I'm Ty Cobb, the crazy one, not Babe Ruth Beloved . . .

CACOETHES: *(Calling after him)* . . . you're a fine *historian*, Kerouac . . . taking down *verbatim* what others do and say . . .

(KEROUAC goes with JAPHY over to PRINCESS. Conversation around CACOETHES becomes inaudible)

KEROUAC: Lots of big-shots around here, Japh . . . no wonder m'buddy Cody stayed away . . .

JAPHY: Don't let Old Cacoethes get at ya, Jacky . . . he cuts everyone to ribbons . . . don't mean a thing, just likes to see the tops of heads fly away . . .

KEROUAC: *(To nobody)* Gimme another slug of that jug . . .

PRINCESS: You want yabyum, Jacky?

KEROUAC: Wha—?

PRINCESS: *(Curling up against JAPHY)* . . . Japhy . . . mmm . . . Princess wants yabyum, some lovely yabyum . . .

JAPHY: *(Laughing happily)* It's not Thursday, Princess . . . yabyum's for Thursday . . . it's important to stick to the discipline. *(Embracing her) If* we can!

SIMON: *(Yelling over)* Japhy is the thunderbolt . . .

JAPHY: (Yelling back joyously) And ants and bees are communists! And trolley cars are bored!

IRWIN: Joe McCarthy is cross-eyed and will suddenly float away!

SIMON: Eat blueberry spies!
    (THEY all laugh)

KEROUAC: (Sour) . . . aw, balls!

JAPHY: (Kind'y) Cheer up, Jack . . . just Zen Lunatics yellin' poems that come into their heads for no reason . . . that's what I like about you and Irwin, strange unexpected acts, giving visions of freedom to everyone — you two guys from the East Coast, which I thought was dead.

IRWIN: We thought the West Coast was dead!

KEROUAC: (Sullen) . . . 'Tsall famous twaddle . . .

JAPHY: What would you say, Jack, if someone asked the question, "Does a dog have the Buddha nature," and they answered, "Woof!"

KEROUAC: I'd say it was a lotta Zen bullshit. . . . I'm a serious Hanayana Buddhist. . . . Wish to Hell Cody had come . . . gotten some sense around here . . .
    (JAPHY throws a flower at KEROUAC)

JAPHY: Woo! That's known as the flower sermon, boy!
    (KEROUAC picks up some food and throws it at JAPHY)

KEROUAC: That's the banana sermon.

IRWIN: That's what I like — these actual signposts to somewhere!

SIMON: Oooh — I wish I could take all this down . . .

JAPHY: You been vexed, Jack, you're lettin' the world drown you in its horseshit.

IRWIN: . . . you can't live in it but there's nowhere else to go.

PRINCESS: Om mani Pahdme Hum.

JAPHY: Rahula! — the Universe chawed and swallowed!

KEROUAC: Sure — we're all excited about being Orientals, and over there real Orientals are reading Darwin and wearin' Western business suits.

JAPHY: East'll meet West. And it's guys like us who started the whole thing. Why did Bodhidharma come from the West?

KEROUAC: I don't care.

JAPHY: *Perfect* answer, absolutely *perfect*. You're already a Zen Master.

SIMON: But not as red as a tomato.

KEROUAC: All you need to know is Sakyamuni's first noble truth: *All life is suffering* . . .

JAPHY: Jack, I do appreciate your sadness about the world but —

KEROUAC: — death's our reward . . . Christ's peace looking down on the heads of his tormentors . . .

PRINCESS: Don't start preaching Christianity, Jack.

KEROUAC: What's wrong with Jesus?

JAPHY: I can just see you on your deathbed, after all those sutras, kissing the cross like some old Karamazov!

KEROUAC: Aw, maybe I'll go to Hollywood and be a famous movie star . . .

(HE *pours another drink.* CACOETHES *comes over, along with one or two of the last remaining guests*)

CACOETHES: Time for us to go . . .
(HE *embraces* IRWIN)
Splendid poem . . . a true beginning.

IRWIN: Thank you, thank you . . .

KEROUAC: The "beginning" was ten years ago at Columbia —

IRWIN: — Jacky —

CACOETHES: — You drink too much, Kerouac . . . you can't become a good bhikku if you're always getting *drronk.*

KEROUAC: Better'n to be "cool" like you, Cacoethes . . . you bourgeois entrepreneur!

SIMON: That's it, Jack — beat him up with your mystical strength!

CACOETHES: Since I can't use your abuse, you can have it back, Kerouac. (HE *exits with his companions*)

KEROUAC: *(Yelling after* CACOETHES) It's the *un*expected poetry I wanna hear . . . *(To* JAPHY) You're the only one out here writes poetry . . . your voice is as tender as a mother's, Japh . . .

IRWIN: *(Hurt)* Didn't you like *my* poem, Jack?

KEROUAC: A'course . . . eloquent rage of old Jewish prophets and all that . . . except the stuff about "granite phalluses" . . .

SIMON: I think Buddhism is getting to know as many people as possible.

PRINCESS: Amen the Thunderbolt
In the Dark Void.

It's yabyum time, yabyum time . . .
   (SHE *sits down facing* SIMON, *puts her arms around his neck*)

SIMON: Oh, this is lovely. (*To* IRWIN) Come on and try it.

IRWIN: I don't know if I can sit cross-legged like that.

JAPHY: It's easier when you take your clothes off.

PRINCESS: (*To* SIMON) Start with the arms . . .
   (SIMON *and* IRWIN *begin to remove their clothing*)

KEROUAC: What the fuck you guys up to now?

IRWIN: Come on, Jack, join us . . .

KEROUAC: I don't wanna have to sit here, look at naked guys!

IRWIN: Oh what's wrong? Jack, you're getting almost sullen!

JAPHY: In Oriental religion there's no question what to do about sex, Jack.

SIMON: Ow! — a mosquito!

IRWIN: A mosquito is bigger than you think!

PRINCESS: A horse's hoof is more delicate than it looks!

IRWIN: Don't step on the aardvark!

SIMON: (*Shivering*) Let's get under the blankets . . .

JAPHY: Horse burps in China are cow moos in Japan!
   (PRINCESS, SIMON, *and* IRWIN *move off to the corner giggling*)

SIMON: We'll wave our pants from stretchers!

IRWIN: We'll bounce babies on our lap!

KEROUAC: *(Yelling after them)* We'll be like death, we'll kneel down to drink from soundless streams.

(SIMON stares at KEROUAC, pop-eyed)

SIMON: *Wow!*

(PRINCESS, SIMON and IRWIN disappear under a mound of blankets)

KEROUAC: Simon the Mad Russian. . . . I hope those guys don't teach me to touch 'em too much . . . I'm fulla hopeless electric snakes . . .

JAPHY: Jack, what you got to do is go climb a mountain with me soon. The secret of climbing, Jacky, is Don't Think. Just dance along. Easiest thing in the world, easier than walking on flat ground.

KEROUAC: Leave all my pills and booze behind, huh? . . . empty and awake . . . be reborn as a teetotalin' bartender . . .
(HE laughs, reaches for wine bottle)
Hey, Japh — tell me another of those hai-*kus*.

JAPHY: *(Smiling)* Well, let's see. . . . How's this?

"The sparrow hops along the veranda,
with wet feet."

That one's by Shiki.
(KEROUAC laughs happily)
You like that, huh? Maybe we'll get our own printing press and make a fat book of hai-*ku* for the booby public.

KEROUAC: Ah, the public ain't so bad, they suffer alot too, you know . . . always readin' about some tar-paper shack burnin' down . . . even the kitty burned . . .

JAPHY: Ah, don't trouble your mind essence.

93

KEROUAC: . . . it's all too pitiful. I ain't gonna rest till I find out why . . . *why*, Japh, *why?*

JAPHY: In pure Tathagata there is no asking of the question "why?"

KEROUAC: Well . . . then nothing really happens.
(HE *brings the wine bottle down on* JAPHY'S *toe.* JAPHY *yelps*)

KEROUAC: See: that didn't happen.

JAPHY: *(Laughing)* You better find a woman, Jack — have half-breed babies, homespun blankets —

KEROUAC: — had hundreds of lover-girls . . . when I was young and . . . not ashamed to ask . . . everyone of 'em I betrayed or screwed in some way. . . . Hey — you know Ruthie? — ever met Ruthie?

JAPHY: Why sure! — ten Ruthies at least!
(THEY *laugh*)

KEROUAC: We oughta go back to the days when men married bears and talked to the buffalo, by Gawd!

JAPHY: Hang on, boy, the ecstasy's general. Somethin' good's coming outta all this.

KEROUAC: That's what Irwin told me ten years ago about the Nickel-O . . . good comin' outta *what?*

JAPHY: Out of all this energy and exuberance focused into the Dharma.

KEROUAC: Ah, balls on that old tired Dharma! . . . I'm too old for young idealisms. I can't even get my books published . . . Cacoethes is probably right about me . . . I'm just a spy in somebody else's body . . .

JAPHY: Jacky-boy, don't give me that . . .

94

KEROUAC: Ah, lousy me, I'hse so tired . . . you know what I'd like? A nice big Hershey bar. Even a little one. A Hershey bar would save my soul . . .

JAPHY: How about moonlight in an orange grove?

KEROUAC: A Hershey bar . . . with nuts . . .

JAPHY: When we gonna climb?

KEROUAC: Huh? — oh yeah . . . I dunno . . . I gotta see Cody . . . gotta find out what's goin' on with Cody . . .
  (HE *starts to doze*)

JAPHY: You'll see in the mountains, Jack, see this vision of a great rucksack revolution, millions of young Americans goin' up the mountains, makin' children laugh and old men glad, makin' young girls happy and old girls happier. Jack, by God, we'll have a fine free-wheeling tribe, have dozens of radiant brats, live like Indians in hogans, eat berries, read —
  (KEROUAC *snores out loud.* JAPHY *stops in mid-sentence and chuckles. Lights dim*)

JAPHY: . . . Yep . . . leapin' the world's ties and sittin' among white clouds . . .

  (*Blackout*)

  (*Cal Tjader music, under*)

SCENE 3

The following week. Pomeray living room. Evening. Glenn Miller's "Moonlight Serenade" is playing on the phonograph.

EVELYN is sitting on the couch with her five-year-old son, TIMMY, who's staring at a light bulb in the ceiling. CODY and KEROUAC, both high, are trying to play along with the Miller record on toy flutes.

KEROUAC: *(Laughing)* . . . trouble, trupple, tripple — whoo! *(To CODY)* . . . see you got my drink!

CODY: *(Teasing, holding KEROUAC's drink out of reach)* You gave all that up in the mountains ya told me!

KEROUAC: Sure, changed m'life — but not m'thirst! . . . special occasion, m'boy . . . big reunion with old hellcat buddy . . .

(CODY gives KEROUAC his drink back)

CODY: What we gotta have is 'nother flute for Evelyn Honeythighs!

EVELYN: *(Good-natured, enjoying their antics)* I'm fine . . . calm down . . . I know it's been five years, *but* —

CODY: — nope, nope, nope . . . gotta have a trio . . .
Timmy, son, where's sister's piccolo, mmm?

(TIMMY *continues to stare at the light bulb*)

. . . child seems absorb-ed in otherworldly aspirations . . .

(CODY *picks up an ocarina, hands it to* EVELYN)

CODY: Here, darlin' . . . you play the sweet potato,
Jack'll play the white piccolo, I'll play the —

EVELYN: — sweetheart, you know I can't play this thing.
Why don't I get you two some coffee?

KEROUAC: . . . assailed from all sides!

CODY: Terrible feelin', man . . . terrible feeling. . . .
But — no time for feelin's, right?

KEROUAC: . . . sure, sure . . . peaceful feelin' on . . .
Mount Hozo-meen . . .

CODY: *(Slight irritation)* You told us 'bout the mountain,
Jacky . . . yass, yass . . . that bee-u-ti-ful Void — uh,
life — Japhy-faphy found in the mountain-laurel
air . . .

KEROUAC: . . . that Japhy's somethin' else . . . why that
cat isn't twenty-four years —

CODY: — just lost mah thought . . . *lost mah thought!*
. . . terrible when people don't . . . listen to ya . . .

KEROUAC: *Terrible!* Christ, yes, man . . . terrible . . .

EVELYN: Coffee, anyone? Last offer.

CODY: . . . uh, no darlin' . . . interfere with the fin-
gerin' of mah cheroot . . .

(KEROUAC *shifts his seat nearer to the phonograph*)

KEROUAC: . . . can't hear . . . guy's so soft . . . can't
get m'thing close enough . . . to hear . . .

CODY: Here. . . sit like this . . .
(HE *positions* KEROUAC)
. . . 'thass 'bout right . . . 'thass right . . . turn a little . . . that side. . . . Shush, now . . . my mighty solo's 'bout to come in . . .

KEROUAC: . . . oh the snake charmer . . .

CODY: Ready! *(Announcing)* We give you — the rape charmer of the Indian plantations!

KEROUAC: . . . sahib, sahib! . . .

TIMMY: Daddy . . . daddy . . .?

CODY: Huh — what, child?

TIMMY: Can we go hiss the villain again?
(EVELYN *and* CODY *laugh*)

KEROUAC: Does that little angel mean *me?*

EVELYN: It's the local theater group I do sets for . . . Cody and I took the kids to see it last night.

CODY: Old 1910 play 'bout villains foreclosin' the mortgage, mustaches, calico tears . . . why we hissed the villains for hours, didn't we, son?

TIMMY: Uncle Jack come, too?

KEROUAC: Why sure, Timmy, I'll go hiss the villains with you anytime.

TIMMY: Thanks, Uncle Jack. (HE *goes back to staring at the light bulb*)

CODY: Timmy, darlin', aren't you ever goin' to bed? Sister's been asleep two hours, son . . .
(TIMMY *doesn't answer*)
What *are* you thinking, man?

KEROUAC: Why, he's high . . . all he wants to do is look at that light . . .

CODY: It's too *strong* . . . bad for his eyes . . .

KEROUAC: "Bad order highs?"

CODY: *Eyes.*

KEROUAC: — eyes, yeah.

EVELYN: It isn't strong, just opens up his irises. I'll put him to bed. *(To* TIMMY*)* C'mon, sweetheart, mommie'll read to you.
(EVELYN *takes* TIMMY *by the hand.* HE *kisses* CODY *good-night)*

CODY: Mmm . . . yummy . . .

TIMMY: *(To* KEROUAC*)* You're not going to go away, Uncle Jack, are you?

KEROUAC: *(Moved)* . . . no, son, no . . . I'll . . . I'll see you in the morning . . .
(TIMMY *breaks into a big grin, then skips off with* EVELYN*)*

CODY: *(Proud)* Now ain't he weird? . . . Ain't that the weirdest kid?

KEROUAC: You sure got a range of graduating golden angels there . . .

CODY: Yass, yass, all truly lovely . . . love 'em more'n I can say . . . only trouble comes when the sun goes down. . . . A man's still got to bat around now and then lookin' for a little ecstasy. . . .
(HE *fiddles with the phonograph. "Them There Eyes" starts playing)*

CODY: . . . that new one I was tellin' you about . . .

KEROUAC: Oh, yeah . . . what she look like?

CODY: Ooh — a gone little body! . . . wanna be sub-beau for another of me beauties, boy?

KEROUAC: Double husbands, eh? — just like the old days . . .

CODY: We'll have us whole reams of Hareems, boy, and we'll call ourselves — "Keromeray," see, hee hee hee . . .

KEROUAC: We gotta be the two most advanced men friends in the world, right?

CODY: Yeah . . . except you Canucks save your spit in your watch pocket.

KEROUAC: What's that mean?

CODY: Oh, goin' around containin' yourself . . . even when you're high, you know?

KEROUAC: *(Evading)* All I hope, Cody, is some day we'll live on the same street with our families and get to be a couple of old-timers together.

CODY: That's right, man — I pray for it completely, mindful of the troubles we had, and the troubles comin'. . . . But you better start makin' that family, boy . . . or *somethin'* . . .

KEROUAC: *(Almost to himself)* . . . stay apart . . . pass through . . . learned that in the mountains . . .

CODY: But *that's* always been your trouble, man.

KEROUAC: . . . no more gnashin' . . . or tears . . .

CODY: Hey, Jack! You hearin' me?

KEROUAC: Huh?

CODY: I'm talkin' about you and me, Jacky . . . or tryin' to . . .

KEROUAC: Oh yeah — double husbands! Sure, I heard ya . . . heard ya . . . steppin' arm'n'arm to the altar . . . *(Drunken laugh)* Hah! But what's ol' Evelyn gonna say 'bout double *wives* . . .
(HE breaks up laughing)

CODY: *(Serious)* You know, Jack, lots of people still care about you . . . I do. . . . But they — well — we get tired of waitin' . . .

KEROUAC: *(Evasive)* Whew, you know — I'm feelin' real drunk . . . feel like an old fool . . .

CODY: Well, I feel pretty foolish, too . . .

KEROUAC: But you feel like a *young* fool!

CODY: Evelyn says I'm an old cuntlapper. *Old!* (CODY *starts to parade around, mimicking a woman)* "Now, Cody, you got to stop bobbing up and down all the time . . . rubbin' that juiceless stubble 'gainst my purty gash, makin' me raw and tender."
(THEY both laugh)

KEROUAC: Aw Cody, ya can't fight nature!

CODY: 'Thass what I said to ol' Irwin the first time!

KEROUAC: — nature made you all cheekbone, impenetrable as steel —

CODY: Yah! — sure fooled me! It was them Nembutals Irwin fed me. Hit me just like that — bam! I was completely outta norm — control . . . was all I could do to hit the bed . . . and that ol' Irwin was jes amazin'! We kept renewin' the supply after that! *(Pause)* You can't trust people once you give 'em exactly what they want.

KEROUAC: I don't get it . . .

CODY: Sure you do. . . . No? . . . Okay. Well, I got better control now than I used to. . . . Man, lissen to this. . . . *(HE changes the record)* This is fine . . . lissen to him walk in . . . the way he blows . . . hear it? Hear him come in there? Whoo, he blows! . . . What I been tryin' to say before about Irwin and me, you know . . .

KEROUAC: *(Listening to the record)* . . . oh, that's fine . . . fine . . .

CODY: . . . it got so, finally, I couldn't stand Irwin to touch me.

KEROUAC: Huh?

CODY: See, only touch me . . . I never been "that way," you know . . . at least, didn't wanna be for too long with Irwin. *(Laughs)* Now with *you*, Jacky . . . it ain't fatal, you know, no matter what your mama told ya . . .

KEROUAC: What's *in* that tea? — I can't understand half of what you're sayin' . . .

CODY: *(Sly)* Wahl, half oughta be enough . . .

KEROUAC: . . . Japhy and me are goin' mountain climbing again next week . . .

CODY: Oh yeah? Wahl good, you got the red face of an outdoorsman already. . . . The thing is, I think your mind is *too* much on the writing, so that you don't have time to really sit down and go into this . . . thing . . .

KEROUAC: *(Trying to laugh it off)* Irwin says they call you The Preacher now . . .

CODY: . . . you gotta watch the shell, man, I been noticin' that in you . . . a shielding, a growin' shell . . .

KEROUAC: Your trouble, Cody, is you think it's a physical universe.

CODY: Yass, yass, sure do!

KEROUAC: Well, I got news for you, nothing has come of something, and that something is Dharmakaya, the body of True Meaning —

CODY: — the hell with all that Buddhist bullshit — lets just cut it out, and *live!*
(HE *goes to the phonograph and puts on Gene Krupa's "Leave Us Leap")*

KEROUAC: All you want to do is run out there and get laid . . . get banged around by samsara. You'll deserve it too, I'll say . . .

CODY: That's not nice. Everybody's tryin' to live with what they got. Your Buddhism's made you mean, Jack . . . *(Pointed)* I'm not as frantic or futile as you sometimes like to believe — so you don't have to look at the other *(Pause)* thing. . . . Now why don't you lissen to this record . . . it's got . . . it's got — everything . . .

KEROUAC: Well, all I want is a shack in the woods . . . wise old Thoreau, sittin' in my cabin. . . . That young Japhy — ten years younger and makin' me look like a fool, forgettin' all the ideals and joys I knew. . . . I'm beginnin' a new life.

CODY: New words, yass . . . looks like new hero comin' in there, too . . . but nuthin' else, Jack, not any new human thing . . . 'cause you won't look at the old ones . . .

KEROUAC: Don't know what's got into you . . .

CODY: What's always been there.

KEROUAC: Well I'll tell you straight, old buddy, I don't like it. You're actin' as weird as Irwin.

CODY: Weird to *you*, 'cause you're tryin' to find your heartbeat on top of some *mountain!* —

KEROUAC: — I know my heart's not in my balls —

CODY: — that's jes what you *don't* know —

KEROUAC: — that's enough, Cody!

CODY: *(Turning to face* KEROUAC *directly, near tears)* Dammit, Jack! I love you, man, you've got to dig that; boy, you've got to know . . . *(EVELYN comes back in)* got to know about our love, you great ol' Jocko Jerk!

EVELYN: *(Softly, concerned for both of them)* . . . I didn't tell you: somebody asked me drive him downtown . . . he was attractive, too . . .

CODY: *(To* KEROUAC*)* Well, we'll all meet in Hell and hatch another plot. . . . *(To* EVELYN*)* Why didn't you, darlin', you might have made . . . five dollars.

EVELYN: *(Laughs)* If only I'd been thinking! Well — you'll be back to work next week, so what the Hell!

KEROUAC: *(Still stunned)* You startin' at the railroad again?

CODY: Naw — gonna wear goggles this time, work like Vulcan at his forge.

KEROUAC: Huh?

EVELYN: He's going to work at Firestone.

CODY: 'Thass right . . . throwin' tires all over the place with mah fantastic strength . . . *(Sarcastic)* while all you got to do is sit around and write little insensible ditties.

KEROUAC: Yeah, big-time writer, that's me . . . stare at the stars, and they stare right back . . .

CODY: Well, I'm just your average dope, go to work and go home, go and try to get a girl, or somethin' . . .

KEROUAC: You can't be average because I've never seen you before . . .

CODY: Why sure — just a normal young kid — Evelyn'll tell ya!

EVELYN: *(Laughs)* Normal! —

CODY: Well, normal-*seeming*, anyway. . . . (HE *starts toward the bathroom)* got to 'scuse me now y'all, gonna take my gorgeous-makin' Joy bubble bath, then get out my new magenty, slamelty jeepster and join the Mongol horde for the Saturday-night Beehive slam . . . hee hee hee . . .

EVELYN: Cody, what in the name of —? Jack's stayin' overnight! You are, aren't you, Jack?

CODY: 'Course he is, darlin' — he promised Timmy. Jack's a man of his word . . . *all* his words. We'll have us a flapjack sausage jamboree come first thing mornin'. But tonight I got to celebrate my new job and this bee-u-tee-ful reunion we jes had . . . seein' you, goo me I'm gushy all over . . . my heart is jess OVER-flowin'! . . . (HE *exits)*

EVELYN: — of all the crazy — ! I haven't seen him *this* wild since —
    (CODY *sticks his head back in)*

CODY: — oh darlin' — I have in the second drawer mantel the LAST, the absolutely LAST yet most perfect of all

black-haired seeded packed tight superbomber joints in the world, which I want you to light up for you and Jack while I'm tossin' bubbles to the ceilin', and while you two talk about me and Irwin and the bed that broke — "Ee-dee-fy his mind with the grand actuality of *FACT*," as dear ol' Will Hubbard used to say . . .
(HE *exits again*)

EVELYN: Poor Jack, I bet you wished you'd stayed wherever you were.

KEROUAC: *(Quietly)* Cody, the Holy Goof.

EVELYN: I get so sick of all this sex business. Here we are, as Edgar Cayce says, all open channels to do good as co-creators with God, and all Cody's thinking about is behinds! Finding Cayce has been good for us, Jack . . . it's quieted him down *some*.

KEROUAC: Yeah, he was tryin' to tell me that . . . or somethin' . . .

EVELYN: You want that joint?

KEROUAC: Sure . . . why not?

EVELYN: Looks like you and me again — just like old times.

KEROUAC: My best pal and my best gal.
(SHE *hands him the joint*)
Another miracle from Edgar Cayce?

EVELYN: Some things we don't joke about, Jack.

KEROUAC: Wish I could figure out which. (HE *lights the joint*)

EVELYN: You and I were made for each other . . . but it's my particular Karma to serve Cody in this particular lifetime. I'll get you in the next one, Jack.

KEROUAC: What? — me running up the eternal halls of Karma tryin' to get away from you?

EVELYN: . . . and what's more, I'll make you very happy. (SHE *puts her arm around* KEROUAC) Ah Jack, it's nice you're here. . . . Why don't you just stay with us awhile and rest?

KEROUAC: *(Sadly)* Too late, I guess . . . *(Almost to himself)* Great Snake of the World coiled out there . . . closer and closer to breakin' through the crust . . .

EVELYN: Huh?

KEROUAC: I will, Evelyn . . . I will . . .

EVELYN: Great Snake of the World?

KEROUAC: *(Trying to be lighter)* That Catholic background of mine . . . gotta watch myself every minute.

EVELYN: Jack, I don't think it's good you live with your mother — you don't mind my saying that, do you?

KEROUAC: Everybody else says it.

EVELYN: You've got your own life to live.

KEROUAC: That's what Ma keeps telling me.

EVELYN: You've done a lot for her, Jack.

KEROUAC: She's done more for me . . . doesn't rant and knock over dressers of makeup.

EVELYN: *I* don't do that! Neither do most women — and you know it!

KEROUAC: No I don't.

EVELYN: Ruthie didn't do it. She was *nice!*

KEROUAC: Her psychiatrist told her a man who loves his mother is the worst scoundrel of all. . . . Naw — my ma just yawns at eleven and goes to bed with her rosary. . . .

EVELYN: Swell, but do you want to live in a monastery?

KEROUAC: Oh, I've heard it all, Evelyn — "Kerouac, you liar! Go out and live with a woman and fight and suffer with her!" — and all the time I'm sittin' there enjoying the sweet silly peace of my mother. . . .

EVELYN: Well, it doesn't seem natural . . .

KEROUAC: What'd Cody tell you about Irwin and the bed?

EVELYN *(Laughing):* Oh, you know . . . a few years back when he and Irwin —

KEROUAC: — Cody told you *that?*

EVELYN: Oh, sure —

KEROUAC: — didn't you . . . *mind* that they were —

EVELYN: — Oh hell, Jack, I learned long ago to take Cody as he is . . . *(Trace of irony)* Just like you said your ma takes you, right?

KEROUAC: Huh? . . . yeah, sure . . .

EVELYN: I thought you and Irwin also . . . I mean —
    (KEROUAC *suddenly jumps up. His chair hits the floor)*
    Jack — what the — what did I say —?
    (CODY *appears upstage.* KEROUAC *doesn't see him)*

KEROUAC: *(Yelling)* They were *lovers!* — not a blow job, Evelyn — *LOVERS!* He told you that, too, I suppose — huh, HUH?
    (CODY *comes downstage)*

EVELYN: Jack, please, I —

108

CODY: — Yeah, ah told her. Got nuthin' to hide, man. Never have. *(Direct, hard) You* got nuthin' to show.

KEROUAC: Is that right? —

EVELYN: — will you both *please* calm down. What in the world started all this —?

CODY: — anything else you wanna say — behind my back?

KEROUAC: Yeah, plenty — plenty to say! Mexico! — "I come, I'm gone! I come, I'm gone!" Just up and leave, up and leave, whenever it suits *you!*

CODY: You never gave me no reason to stay.

KEROUAC: . . . never shoulda come back here . . . too late . . . shoulda known it was too late . . .

CODY: I think maybe that's right, ol' buddy . . .

EVELYN: It's *not* right! We're Jack's oldest friends! You *belong* here, Jack!

CODY: Jack don't belong nowhere . . . doesn't want to . . . rather sit around wonderin' where to go . . . and all the time it's right in front of him . . .

KEROUAC: *(Yelling)* All *you* ever want is to get *laid!*
    (TIMMY, *frightened, appears at the doorway in his bathrobe)*

TIMMY: — Daddy?

CODY: — no, son! — go back, son! *(To* KEROUAC, *furious)* See what you done, man, scared my little boy, scared my little Timmy . . .

KEROUAC: — laid, man — *LAID!*

EVELYN: *(To* TIMMY*)* C'mere, darlin' . . .
(TIMMY *runs over to* EVELYN. SHE *holds him)*

KEROUAC: I'm sure he's seen worse! *Lots* worse, lots
worse . . .

CODY: *(Blowing up)* Get outta here, man! — *get outta
here!*

EVELYN: Cody, please . . . you're frightening Timmy . . .

CODY: *(Yelling)* Buddhist bullshitter — go daddle with
your *kidneys!*

TIMMY: Is Uncle Jack the villain, should we hiss Uncle
Jack?

EVELYN: Shush. Timmy darlin' . . .

KEROUAC: *(Screaming)* Cunt's the one thing you care
about — CUNT! YOU FUCKING ETERNAL PIECE
OF MEAT!
(CODY *goes for* KEROUAC, *lands a hard punch on his
jaw.* CODY *then quickly retreats, turns his back,
pounds one fist into the other in frustrated despair.*
HE *grabs up* TIMMY *in his arms)*

TIMMY: *(Crying)* . . . bad daddy . . . hiss, hiss, bad daddy . . . bad daddy . . . hiss . . . hiss . . .	CODY: *(To* EVELYN*)* . . . get him out . . . get him out of here . . . (HE *exits with* TIMMY)

KEROUAC: . . . breakin' through . . . the Snake's breakin' through . . .
(The lights dim.)

EVELYN: *(Crying softly)* . . . Jack . . . oh, Jack . . .
(SHE *exits)*
(KEROUAC *remains alone in spot, sprawled at edge
of the stage)*

KEROUAC: . . . hissing . . . the Snake, hissing . . . when you die, you won't know . . . can't pretend you won't know . . .

(Lights dim to out)

SCENE 4

KEROUAC, *in spot, staggers to his feet. We're back on the television sound stage, 1958 — same setting as at end of act one, scene 1.*

KEROUAC: . . . Call themselves poets
Call themselves Kings
Call themselves Free . . .
Call themself me . . .

(Lights up full. CAMERON *crosses the sound stage on his way out of the studio.* HE *stops when he sees* KEROUAC)

CAMERON: *(Sarcastic)* Certainly a "pleasure" having you on the show tonight, *Mr.* Kerouac. *(*HE *exits)*

KEROUAC: What am I doin' here? . . . *(Yelling after* CAMERON) Is there some way I'm *supposed* to feel? . . . *(*TV CREW MEMBER *enters)*

CREW MEMBER: Mr. Kerouac, there's someone here to see you. *(Annoyed)* The TV studio is closing. *(*HE *exits)*

KEROUAC: Huh? Oh yeah, sure . . .

*(A woman [*RUTH*] appears just outside the circle of lights)*

WOMAN (RUTH): *(Gently)* . . . Jack? . . .

KEROUAC: . . . huh? Who's that?
   (RUTH *steps into the light)*

WOMAN: It's me, Jack . . . Ruthie . . .

KEROUAC: Ruthie?! — It must be them DTs they keep
   warnin' me about . . .

RUTH: *(Grinning)* No, it's me. . . . How are you, Jack?

KEROUAC: But I don't —! I mean, what the Hell are you
   doin' here in New York?

RUTH: I live here! I saw the program, I was in the studio
   audience . . . I almost didn't come backstage . . .

KEROUAC: I showed those punks, huh? All those big
   professors burping with "rash-on-ality"!

RUTH: I liked that one fella . . . but you made some
   good points, Jack.

KEROUAC: That Jewish Wiman guy's the biggest bastard
   . . . *(Shakes his head with self-disgust)* Ooh . . . I'm
   gettin' to sound as bigoted as the old man, cursin' out
   Jews and Neigres. . . . Shit, Saint Augustine was a
   spade — I know that! . . . Ah, Ruth, I usta like *every-*
   body . . . it's all happened for me too late . . . the
   saints are gone, all gone . . . I talk to waiters only
   now . . .

RUTH: Jack, you're *famous!* Everybody's talking about
   you!

KEROUAC: . . . yeah, kids writin' me letters, knockin' on
   the door . . . scares Ma half to death —

RUTH: You still live with your mother?

KEROUAC: *(Going right on)* — they all think I'm twenty-
   five, set to hitchhike off with 'em, follow some great

113

red line straight across America. . . . Shit, it's 1958, I'm lucky I can make it to the neighborhood bar. . . . I'm King of the Beats, but I ain't no Beatnik. *(Chuckles grimly)* There ain't no more Road . . . just like there ain't no more Cody. . . . *(Pause. Guiltily)* Ever hear from him?

RUTH: Yes . . . we write. *(Shyly)* Don't you, uh, haven't you written to him, Jack?

KEROUAC: *(Ignoring her)* What a bum rap! — two to life for dealin'! Them fuckin' narcos! Cody never pushed drugs! — anyone could tell 'em that! — The reefers were for his friends, thass all, all for his friends . . .

RUTH: He's been tryin' to get Evelyn to sell the house for bail money . . . she won't do it, says it's all she and the kids got . . .

KEROUAC: — Where's that Ga-damn bottle?! Hadda stash the sauce back here, Ruthie, those old farts din wanna "shock the viewin' public" — hah!

(HE staggers around looking for the bottle, then swigs from it)

Cauterize my wounds, Ruthie m'gal! . . . Ma won't let me bring no gal back to the house — 'less I *marry* her — ha! . . . got her a nice lil house. Used up all the bread, but what the hell — got *five* books comin' out this year and next, *five!* Wrote most of 'em years ago a'course . . . best one's *Doctor Sax*, though Irwin don't think so — aw, what's he know, all wrapped up in Simon and takin' his clothes off every time he recites more'n two lines of his own poetry, and gettin' all political about the BOMB and Joe McCarthy and — *(Repentant)* Aw. I don't mean that. Irwin's the only loyal friend I got, even if he is a wolf in sheep's clothing. . . . *(Scornful, imitating)* Now we got that "cool" shit — "Oh, it's a wig, man . . . a real gas . . . like you know, wow! crazy!" *(Disgust)* . . . And claiming *me* as their spiritual father — that's a joke! . . .

RUTH: Now come on, confess, Jack —

KEROUAC: Huh?

RUTH: — admit you like being famous *just a little!*

KEROUAC: Wanna know somethin', Ruthie? Hah? Hah?

RUTH: Sure, Jack . . .

KEROUAC: *(Leaning down and "whispering")* Truth is — I'd rather be *thin* than famous!
    *(*THEY *laugh)*

RUTH: You're not fat.

KEROUAC: Wha—?! You don't remember my fightin' Football Hero trim? Not an ounce of flesh on me. . . . Now I couldn't even give ya a baby. . . . 'Cause of my thrombophlebitis — piss goin' the wrong way.

RUTH: What makes you think I want a baby?

KEROUAC: Oh you always did. . . . Yup — I'm the end of a strong line. . . .

RUTH: Jack, we went through all that years ago. . . . I'm grateful I can take care of *me* now. Don't want any other mouth to feed. . . .

KEROUAC: You still got mad blue eyes, you know . . . little flutter to 'em, too. . . . Aw — it's all high school stuff anyway! . . . Hey, Ruthie — how come soft women like hard hairy men, huh? 'Tsamazing — where's the beauty in all that hardness?

RUTH: Look at Cody and you'll know . . .

KEROUAC: *(Resentful)* You always did like him. . . . What he think of the book, huh? I hear he gets lots

115

of fan mail addressed to "Dean Moriarity, Hero of *On The Road*" *(Laughs)* Put old Cody on the map, right?! Don't know why he blames me . . . what the Hell is there to blame *me* for, huh?

RUTH: No one blames you, Jack . . .

KEROUAC: *(Flaring)* — don't tell me! I heard! I heard what Cacoethes and them other pricks in California are sayin' — that they picked Cody up because I had him takin' all that dope in the book! Shit! — they didn't pick *me* up, they didn't pick up Will or Irwin!

RUTH: . . . nobody blames you, Jack . . . really . . .

KEROUAC: . . . never knew any limits, that was his trouble . . . you pay through the nose for short-lived shows . . .

RUTH: That's why we loved him . . . there's never been anybody so alive. . . . Jack, do you think you oughta go on drinking? I mean, you've —

KEROUAC: — I knew up in the mountains, Ruthie, when Japhy took me up the mountains. . . . I *knew* everything made sense, was *all right* just as it was. . . . *(Sad)* If I could only hold on to what I *knew* . . . *(Subdued)* Maybe I am drinkin' too much . . .

RUTH: My God, Jack, you haven't stopped . . .

KEROUAC: It keeps me from thinkin' too much, like I'm doin' now. *(Flaring)* I think you're hung up on Cody — I think you always *were* hung up on him! *(Pause)*

RUTH: *(Dignified)* I care about Cody, Jack. I pray for him every day.

KEROUAC: *(Sarcastic)* Oh — that's nice!

RUTH: — and I'll go on praying for him as long as he's in prison —

KEROUAC: . . . good . . . good . . .

RUTH: *(Angry)* — and if you wanna make fun of it, go right ahead . . . maybe if you were to write to Cody nowadays or go see him, you could pass on some of that wisdom you're so full of . . . *(Starts to cry)* God, Jack — you're . . . you're not *sensitive!*

KEROUAC: Oh Ruthie — oh no, don't do that — Ruthie, no — what did I *do?* — what did I do this time, huh —? *(HE tries to comfort her. SHE moves away)*

RUTH: *(More subdued)* . . . leave me alone . . . leave me alone . . .

KEROUAC: . . . I try not to hurt anything . . . really, I try . . .

RUTH: Oh Jack . . . you strange man . . . all these years, and I still don't understand what —

KEROUAC: — would you feel better if you let me hold you, even though I don't deserve it . . . ? *(RUTH sobs and goes to him. THEY embrace)*

RUTH: . . . "don't deserve it"? . . . who ever told you such a terrible thing . . . ?

KEROUAC: I dunno . . . everybody I guess . . . I dunno what I did wrong or when I did it —

RUTH: You withhold your love, Jack. That's what you *do* — what you've always done . . .

KEROUAC: I guess I don't want it . . .

RUTH: But you *do.* Saying you don't is part of the same thing.

KEROUAC: You don't know. I'm a strange guy now . . .

RUTH: You could make some *effort,* damn it — instead of all those vague words, big philosophies . . .

KEROUAC: . . . all my goddam fault . . .

RUTH: . . . oh, God . . .

KEROUAC: . . . always sabotagin' great plans to be kind to livin' things . . .

RUTH: No, it's nobody's fault . . . it's nobody's fault, darlin' . . .

KEROUAC: Why did you call me "darlin' "?

RUTH: Because I care about you . . .

KEROUAC: Aw, you've been assigned by Cody to get me to marry you so he'll get all my money.

RUTH: That's a bad joke. . . .

KEROUAC: I guess it's the Nickel-O.

RUTH: Huh?

KEROUAC: . . . I'm feelin' sick . . . something wrong with me . . . I wanta go home and die with my cat . . .
>   (RUTH *puts her arms around him, tries to comfort him*)
>   . . . don't do it Ruthie, don't do it Ruthie don't do it, Ruthie . . .

RUTH: . . . please, Jack . . . please take it easy . . . let me help you a little . . . please . . . just try to give a little . . .

KEROUAC: . . . I can't . . . got nuthin' to give that'll help anybody . . .

RUTH: . . . please try, Jack . . .

KEROUAC: *(Blowing up) I CAN'T!* . . . it's the secret poisoning society . . . big molecular comedown, like Irwin warned . . . all the atoms fallin' apart . . .

118

RUTH: *(Giving up)* Okay . . . okay . . .

KEROUAC: What are you givin' me that bleak look for —
like I was dead?

RUTH: You want to be left out from everything . . . you
always have . . . rather stay royal drunk and feel sorry
for yourself.

KEROUAC: That's right — cover the earth on, do the
honors! . . . And what'm I suppos'ta do with the ter-
rors I see — huh? huh?! Got any big Final Statements
for that?

RUTH: You'll sleep 'em off.

KEROUAC: Ha — shows what you know!

RUTH: I've had my share, Jack. You got no monopoly
on suffering. . . .

KEROUAC: You're just mad 'cause I didn't stay with
ya. . . .

RUTH: Maybe . . .

KEROUAC: . . . women own the earth, women own
heaven, too . . . it's a tyranny . . .

RUTH: I'm going, Jack . . . going home . . .

KEROUAC: Why should you care, anyway . . .?

RUTH: . . . do what you like, I don't care . . .

KEROUAC: . . . Ma was right . . . it'll all drive me nuts.
(THEY're at the exit)
. . . So whatta we gonna do with our lives?

RUTH: Just watch 'em I guess . . .

KEROUAC: You gonna be okay?

RUTH: I've been okay for some time.

KEROUAC: Salvation's only for little kitties, I 'spose . . .
(HE *starts to cry.* RUTH *involuntarily starts toward him, then stops herself*)
. . . oh ti Tykey, aide mué . . . throwin' it all away, huh Ruthie? . . . just throwin' it away . . .

RUTH: Jack, I don't know what to say anymore . . . I guess you and I said it all years ago . . .

KEROUAC: . . . do you hate me?

RUTH: . . . no . . .

KEROUAC: *(Doing a drunken little jig)* . . . well, do you still love me then?

RUTH: I love the man who wants to know. . . .

KEROUAC: Yeah, well . . . *(Raising the bottle)* Here's to the rosy Figury . . . that's what Cody usta call the Future . . .

RUTH: Good-bye, Jack . . . I'll pray for you . . .

(Lights out)

SCENE 5

Living room of KEROUAC's *house in Lowell, 1969.*
Twilight. Architecture and furnishings reminiscent
of the living room of his boyhood home, but a
"middle-class" version a la Sears Roebuck — plastic
dinette set, maple and chintz. The same religious
objects (statue of Sainte Thérèse, etcetera) as in act
one, scene 6. And one prominent new addition: a
large oil painting of Pope Paul — almost in cartoon
style, with huge blue eyes. A TV set in the corner is
on, but not the sound.

KEROUAC *sits over his typewriter at the dining*
room table. HE's *aged considerably: his hair is thin*
and askew; HE *has a large paunch; his air — like*
EMIL *in act one, scene 6 — is one of bewildered de-*
feat, his tone bellowing (though sometimes in a
self-mocking way). HE *wears a bright Hawaiian*
sport shirt. The top button on his pants is open, his
belly hanging out.

HE *takes the page out of the typewriter, throws it*
into the wastebasket in disgust, and goes to the

refrigerator for a beer, limping slightly as HE *walks.* HE *wears battered old work shoes.*

The doorbell rings. KEROUAC *looks confused, frightened, as if* HE *might bolt. Then* HE *gets angry.*

KEROUAC: *(Muttering)* . . . 'nother fuckin' pest! I swear I'm gonna —!
(Tinkle of a handbell from the back room)

KEROUAC: *(Yelling upstage)* — Yeah, Ma — I heard it! Probably the groceries! Tell Stella I'll get it!
*(*HE *goes to the door and opens it.* JOEY ROSE *is standing there — young, bearded, wearing a jean jacket, ragged but elegant pants and fancy shoes; his manner is gentle and quiet.* IRWIN *is "hiding" behind him.* IRWIN *has changed a great deal physically:* HE's *almost bald, is much heavier, has a full beard. His manner is far more settled and composed than when* HE *was younger)*

JOEY: *(As* IRWIN *whispers the words to him)* Excuse me, but is this the home of Old El Jacko, Champeen Walking Saint? . . .

KEROUAC: What the Hell do you — (HE *catches sight of* IRWIN) Holy shit! — no, it can't be! IRWIN! — Good Christ! what in the Hell are you —?

IRWIN: *(Tenderly)* — yes, it's me, Jack. *(Fingering his beard)* Didn't know if you'd recognize me . . .

KEROUAC: Well don't this beat everything! . . . *(Smiling broadly)* You

KEROUAC: *(continuing)*
crazy bastard! *(Cocking his head toward the back room)* Don't you remember the near riot the last time you —

IRWIN: — we're on our way to a reading at Amherst . . . passed the highway sign for Lowell and thought, "Well, can't hurt to —"

(KEROUAC gives him a huge bear hug)

KEROUAC: — you old cockroach . . . you old cockroach, you . . .

(THEY hang on to each other in a fierce embrace. Agitated tinkle of a handbell sounds from the back room. KEROUAC jumps)

KEROUAC: Yeow! — it's as if she could see right in here! Lissen — hang on! — I'll tell her it's Alex — Stella's brother — that we're gonna have a few beers and watch the Green Bay game — *don't you go away!*
(HE hurries off to the back room)

IRWIN: *(Teary)* . . . ol' Jack . . . God bless him . . .

JOEY: *(Stunned)* . . . That's . . . *that's* Jack Kerouac?

IRWIN: Yes . . . the legendary Beat himself . . . Ah, you should have seen him twenty years ago . . . handsomest man in America . . . fell in love with him at first sight . . .

JOEY: Wow! . . . I mean . . . he doesn't look like what I expected . . .

IRWIN: The years have been hard on him . . . I'm a little shocked myself. . . . Be careful, Joey, he's a sensitive man, and his mother doesn't like me in the house . . . *(Chuckles)* threw me out the last time!
(KEROUAC *comes bouncing back in*)

KEROUAC: All set! All set! . . . She's listenin' to Symphony Sid. . . . Come in, dammit, come in! You want a beer? Hah? Some whiskey?

IRWIN: Jack, this is Joey. He's a young poet from Oregon.

KEROUAC: Oregon, huh? That's where Japhy was from . . . the mountains of Oregon. . . . Well, sit down, dammit . . . *(Beaming)* Irwin Goldbook — you old son of a bitch! (KEROUAC *goes to the refrigerator and comes back with two six-packs of beer*) My God — how many years has it been?

IRWIN: Let's see, not counting the time your mother threw me out —?
(THEY *laugh*)
. . . almost five years, in 'sixty-four when Cody came through New York with Kesey and the Pranksters. . . .
(KEROUAC *scowls*)

KEROUAC: Some scene that was . . .

IRWIN: *(Sad)* I thought it would be a happy reunion. . . .

KEROUAC: *(Serious)* Yeah, well you didn't behave well, Irwin, drapin' an American flag over my shoulders like that . . .

IRWIN: I meant it satirically . . . a mistake . . .

KEROUAC: That's no way to treat the flag, Irwin . . . it's not some old rag you play around with. . . . Never mind! Let's forget all that now. . . . Here, have some beer . . .

JOEY: No thanks, sir. I . . . I don't drink . . .

KEROUAC: Figures . . . doesn't mix with the LSD, right?
— the "higher consciousness"?

IRWIN: LSD's a useful tool, Jack, I've taken it many times.

KEROUAC: Oh you — you'll do anything! Don't worry! —
I tried it. Made me dippy with visions . . . I got
enough visions . . . *(Winces)* Ow! *(Holds his stomach)*
. . . I got a goddam hernia . . . belly button's poppin'
out. That's why I'm dressed like this. . . . Well, I got
no place to go . . . I'm glad to see ya . . . gets kinda
lonesome here sometimes . . .
   (JOEY reaches into his shoulder bag)
Lissen, kid, you're not gonna take any pictures, are ya?
'Cause if you take any pictures of me, I'll kick your
ass, you hear?
   *(JOEY draws his hand out of the bag to reveal that
it's holding a paperback)*

JOEY: I don't have a camera, Mr. Kerouac —

KEROUAC: — and don't call me *Mister*, see! *(Seeing the
paperback, repentant)* Aw — I'm sorry! I don't even
know ya, and here I am yellin' at ya already. . . . It's
just that — you gotta understand — all kinds of people
come by here pestering me . . . that's why we came
back to Lowell. *(Growling)* I'm sick and tired of kids
trying to pour out their lives into me so I'll jump up
and down and say "yes yes that's right!" . . . little
farts of conformity. *(To JOEY)* Pretty fancy shoes you
got there . . . never seen a poet dressed like that before. . . .

IRWIN: It's the new underground, Jack . . . they like
soft and beautiful things . . .

KEROUAC: Yeah, I heard — Beat Dandies, like their rock-
star heroes. . . . Those weird new eyes of the second

part of the century. . . . *(To* JOEY*)* I'll bet you don't even know who won the Preakness this year, hah? Oh, I know — you got the military-industrial complex to worry about.

IRWIN: Their manners are gentle, too, Jack. . . . You'd like them if you knew them better. . . .

KEROUAC: Well, you always did keep up, Irwin. . . . I hear you've been Om-ing your way from coast to coast. Me, I just stay the same, let all the fads wear themselves out around me . . . *(Gesturing toward the TV screen)* . . . everything gone in the mosaic mesh of television . . . can't stand the sound, but the images keep me company . . .

JOEY: *(Embarrassed)* I like *your* shoes, Mr. — uh — sir — I mean, well, they're like the ones I used to wear in high school. . . . I don't suppose you'd want to, I mean, it would be a real honor for me if you'd maybe want to exchange those for my —

KEROUAC: *(Bellowing)* — Wha—! You crazy? Can't you see me prancin' around Danny's Bar in pale leather PUMPS! — Whoa!

JOEY: *(Crestfallen)* . . . I'm sorry, I didn't mean to . . . it's just that I dug the —

IRWIN: — Joey was high-jump champ in high school, Jack, once made a leap of six-feet-nine . . . right, Joey?

KEROUAC: C'mon! Little fella like that? Who you tryin' to kid?

JOEY: Irwin, I think I'll . . . why don't I wait in the car, or maybe walk around a little . . . you two must have alot to talk about, it's hard to do that with a stranger . . .

KEROUAC: *(Softening)* Oh, that's okay Joey. *(Guffaws)* Strangers never shut *us* up, right Irwin?

IRWIN: *(To* JOEY*)* Go ahead, Joey, if you'd feel more comfortable . . . I won't be long.
*(*JOEY *goes to the door)*

KEROUAC: Now there's no call for that, Joey . . . just sit down and have a beer . . .

JOEY: *(Simple, unpetulant)* No, I'd rather not . . . but thanks anyway . . . *(At the door)* Your books have meant alot to me, Mr. Kerouac . . . to my friends, too . . . I just wanted to thank you for writing them. . . .

KEROUAC: *(Softer)* Oh yeah? . . . well, thanks, Joey, thanks . . . I'm always here, you know . . . don't have a phone, but . . . well, if you're in the area again sometime, drop in and say hello. . . .

JOEY: Much appreciate that. Thank you. *(*HE *exits)*

IRWIN: He means it — about your books, Jack. He's one of the sweetest guys I've ever known . . . a kind of joyful observer . . . reminds me alot of you, back at Columbia . . . on a sort of pilgrimage . . .

KEROUAC: Well, his eyes look clear . . . a lot of faith in his eyes. . . . Aw, Irwin, tell him I'm sorry . . . there's . . . there's so much bullshit everywhere . . .
*(*HE *reaches for a small medicine vial with a plastic cap, snaps it open and drinks from it)*

IRWIN: What's that?

KEROUAC: It's so I won't spill it. *(Shaking the vial)* Johnny Walker Red. Call me Mister Boilermaker.
*(*IRWIN *reaches down and picks up a magazine off the floor)*

IRWIN: *National Review.* Your reading habits have changed.

KEROUAC: Buckley's saying *exactly* what we said twenty years ago: the sacredness of the *individual*, the —

IRWIN: — he means *some* individuals: whites, males, heterosexuals —

KEROUAC: — there's plenty to be said for the old America.

IRWIN: We fought *all* the authorities, Jack, *all* the imposed pieties. And the kids today are, too.

KEROUAC: Yeah, yeah I've heard ya on TV . . . you've always been a good talker, Irwin, too good a talker — that's your trouble. . . .

IRWIN: *(Affectionately)* You used to be a good listener.

KEROUAC: Well I'll tell *you* something! The insane things being done in this country — riots, hoodlumism! It's enough to make Atlas drop his load!

IRWIN: *(Good-natured)* You always did need a hero. I guess Buckley's the new candidate. *(Charmingly)* I wish it could have been me.

KEROUAC: Aw — you're too accessible.
     (THEY *laugh*)

IRWIN: It's funny, Jack: the words you say and the man inside don't match. And the louder you yell, the less they match.

KEROUAC: Still analyzing, huh? — I'm glad some things don't change. Well, truth is, I'm a "Bippie" — the man in the middle. As I get older I get more . . . genealogical.

IRWIN: Are you writing?

128

KEROUAC: Oh sure. Gotta keep the Jewish literary mafia busy . . . still calling me a cut-rate Thomas Wolfe, the going phrase for mah "oeuvre" . . . *(Laughs)* Fuck'em. *(Nodding towards the portrait of the Pope)* I still got those big blue eyes smilin' at me. Painted that myself, you know. May start a whole new career. Hah! Have some more beer. . . .

IRWIN: No, Jack, thanks. *(Looks at his watch)* I have to go soon. The reading's at eight.

KEROUAC: Wait! — Whadda they áll up to? Haven't heard from anybody in years.

IRWIN: Oh, we're practically the Establishment. They're starting to call Will one of the giants.

KEROUAC: Giant buggerer! Academy Award for Sodomy Significance!

IRWIN: Don't mimic your friends, Jack. It doesn't become you.

KEROUAC: Hah! — like what Will once said to me! "If I didn't know you," he said, "I'd swear you were the craziest piece of rough trade that ever walked." Hah!

IRWIN: Will was always pithy.

KEROUAC: You were both pretty *(Deliberately mispronouncing)* "pissy" when you wanted me to be trade for you. *(Patting his belly)* Don't want me now, do you. You got all those young high-jump champs followin' you around . . .

IRWIN: You're still a handsome man, Jack. And I still love you. Just as I love Simon. We separate, but always come back.

KEROUAC: Cody, too, right?

IRWIN: *(Surprised)* Yes.

KEROUAC: I got my rhythm from Cody, my Okie rhythm, see. "Now, look h'yar, boy. I'm gonna tell you what, see" — Cody, great Midwest poolroom saint alive . . .

IRWIN: *(Gently)* Jack, you *did* hear the news?

KEROUAC: Oh yeah — Evelyn called me. They *say* he's dead . . .

IRWIN: In Mexico, by the railroad tracks . . . froze to death by the tracks . . . booze and barbiturates . . .

KEROUAC: *(Angry)* — yeah, yeah, I heard all about it! Tell ya somethin', Irwin: it's bullshit — he's hidin', don't want to come back to the old routine . . .

IRWIN: Jack, it's true. I know people who were with him when —
(KEROUAC takes out the crystal)

KEROUAC: — it's still glistening, see . . .

IRWIN: What is?

KEROUAC: . . . present Cody once gimme when we were on a mountain road, hitchin' . . . a little crystal. Hmmm — near twenty-five years ago! . . . I had the damndest dream about him — just the other night. We were takin' craps together side by side in a double crapper. Cody is talkin' about an actor as I wipe myself with the paper. "But you know he's queer," Cody says, "he blows the Kings." And I have my part on my lap, and I can feel the swelling, so I hurry to wipe up ere it's a pole, but get all tangled in the wiping and get some crap in my mouth . . . here I am trying to remove the hunk of dreamcrap from my mouth which is also full of toilet paper — I'd wiped *it*, instead of below — and Cody's talkin' away about *(Breaks up with "laughter")* blow jobs! Crazy, huh? . . . *(Singing)*

"I'm romantic
And strictly frantic
I love those old-fashioned times."

Hah! Better lose some weight . . . You ever see that poem I wrote to you?

IRWIN: I think so . . .

KEROUAC: Ah! Didn't read it, huh?

IRWIN: I did.

IRWIN: I *did* read it — I *wrote* to you about it!

KEROUAC: Some old friend —! Well, I'm a loyal person, too, and got nuthin' left to be loyal about . . .
(KEROUAC stumbles around, finds the poem)

Here — *(Reading)*
"Poem dedicated to Irwin Goldbook" . . .

KEROUAC: Oh — you did? Good! Then we can sing along together — give it that real old-time feelin'. *(Reading)* ". . . prap-rot-rort-mort-prot-lort-snort —" *(Mugging, grinning)* C'mon, Irwin!

IRWIN: I forget it . . .

KEROUAC: Aw — and you swore you'd never forget me! Well — lissen then, and you tell me if you ever heard a better poem about gettin' sucked off! *(Reading)*

". . . loll my wildmoll — roll my luck —
lay my cashier gone amuck —
suck my lamp pole, raise the bane,
    hang the traitor

    inside my brain
    Fill my pail well,
  ding my bell, smile for the ladies,
      come from hell."

  (HE *laughs uproariously, reaches for the vial of scotch*)

IRWIN: *Definitely* the best of its kind! I wish you had more competitors.

KEROUAC: Most guys wanta hide that sorta experience. . . . Not me . . . up front with everything . . . jes like Cody . . .

IRWIN: I'm glad you wrote about it. That took courage.

KEROUAC: Naw — I figured nobody would understand it. And if they did, they wouldn't believe it!

IRWIN: Why the lines "hang the traitor/inside my head"?

KEROUAC: Oh no you don't! I know what you're up to — want me to join Fags Anonymous — right? Alkie Anonymous, maybe, but that other stuff — no. You brought out all of that that was ever in me — maybe more than was in me.

IRWIN: *(Smiling)* We all have an endless supply.

KEROUAC: Said the old man as he kissed the alligator!
  (THEY *laugh*)

KEROUAC: Remember when you me and Cody goofed about dirty assholes?
  (IRWIN *giggles*)
(Laughing) — Huh? Huh? When we hit on the fantastically simple truth that everybody in America was walking around with a dirty ass — but *everybody* — the President of the United States, movie stars, executives, great engineers —

IRWIN: *(Laughing harder)* — stop it, Jacky, stop! —

KEROUAC: *(Piling it on)* — yeah! All those lawyers with silk shirts and neckties, yet there's something gnawing at them, something's wrong, they know something's wrong, they don't know *JUST WHAT!* They were callin' us filthy unwashed beatniks and we were the only ones walkin' around America with — *(IRWIN joins him in shouting the last two words)*

KEROUAC and IRWIN: — *clean azzoles!*
(As they break up in laughter, GABRIELLE appears from the back room. SHE walks with a cane and is able to force out only a word or two of speech. STELLA KEROUAC is trying to restrain her. STELLA is a plain-looking woman about five years older than KEROUAC; her manner is quiet, patient, good-natured, deferential. GABRIELLE is ringing her handbell furiously, her eyes ablaze)

GABRIELLE: *(Strangled, hissing)* . . . chien . . . chien . . . en culotte . . . vas! . . . vas! . . . plein . . . d'marde! . . . vas! . . . Out! . . . vas! . . . FBI! Out! . . . FBI! plein! . . . d'marde! . . .

KEROUAC: Ma! Oh, fer krissakes! . . . Ma, it's okay . . . Irwin was in the neighborhood . . .

STELLA: Jack, I'm sorry . . . she carried on so, I had to . . . I tried to turn up the radio but . . .

IRWIN: I'm sorry, Mrs. Kerouac . . . I only stopped in for a minute . . . I'll be going . . . I'll be going . . .

(KEROUAC rushes up to GABRIELLE, turns her toward the back room)

KEROUAC: Stop, Ma! Stop! . . . You can't talk like that to Irwin! Ma, he's my oldest friend! . . . The doctor, Ma, be calm! . . . It's all right, he's going, he's going! . . .

(KEROUAC and GABRIELLE exit)

STELLA: I'm sorry, Mr. Goldbook, but I think you'd better —

IRWIN: — yes, I was on my way anyway.

STELLA: She's been terribly ill.

IRWIN: I'd heard about the stroke. . . . You, of course, are Stella.

STELLA: Yes.

IRWIN: You . . . you and Jack weren't married when I was here last time . . . but I'd heard about that, too.

STELLA: We were married right after Gabrielle's stroke.

IRWIN: I'm glad he — I'm glad they — have you, Stella. Please . . . please take good care of him. . . .

STELLA: I waited thirty years to do just that. We knew each other in high school, you know . . . from a distance . . .

(KEROUAC rushes back in)

KEROUAC: — Irwin! Ah! . . . I was afraid you'd gone . . . What a mess! Boy, that old dame can still carry on, can't she? It's true what they say: Canucks learn nuthin', forget nuthin'. . . . Stella, go back there to her . . . I think she's okay . . . tell her Irwin's gone . . . put her into the bed . . .

STELLA: All right . . .

134

IRWIN: Good-bye, Stella . . .

STELLA: . . . good-bye — Mr. Goldbook. *(SHE exits)*

KEROUAC: Jesus, Irwin, helluva way to end a reunion! What can I tell ya? She's a great old lady — a goddam saint, lying back there, never complainin' . . . but on the subject of you — well, we're all a little crazy, as I guess you know . . .

IRWIN: I understand . . . I have to go anyway, Jack.

KEROUAC: Hey — wait!
(HE pulls off his shoes and hands them to IRWIN)
Here — give these to Joey. Tell him . . . aw, I dunno, tell him I think Oregon's terrific . . . that I love mountains — one place I was ever at peace . . .
(THEY embrace)

IRWIN: I love you, Jack . . . if only you knew what a good man you are . . .
(IRWIN exits)

KEROUAC: *(To himself)* . . . Come back and see me . . . please . . . *(Calling out through the screen door)* You're a greater poet than ever! — you're really going now! — don't stop! — remember to write without stopping — I wanna hear *(Trailing off)* . . . what's at the bottom of your mind . . . I love you, too, Irwin. . . .
(HE starts to sob. STELLA comes out of back room)
. . . can't go back . . . can't go forward . . . our fathers raised us to . . . sit on nails . . . *(Suddenly yelling)* Stella! Hey! Turn the God-damn mus— *(Turns and sees her standing there quietly)* Oh . . . turn the goddam music up, willya . . .

STELLA: I'm afraid it will wake her. She's quiet now . . . Jack — he really mustn't come here again. That kind of excitement, she can't afford to —

KEROUAC: — lissen, who pays the rent here, *dammit?* I pay the rent! I'm the guy who bought us *(Bitter laugh)* this thirty-thousand-dollar mansion, as Dorothy Kilgallen calls it in her column. Hah! If I paid thirty thousand for this shithole, I sure got cheated. . . .
(HE gets the bottle of scotch)

STELLA: It's time to eat, Jack . . . I made a stew out of —

KEROUAC: *(Lashing out)* — you eat it! . . . *(Quieter)* I'm sad and I'm — *drunk!* I wanna see . . . for some reason I have a tremendous sad desire and reason just to be with, just to see . . . *(Trails off)*

STELLA: See who, Jack?

KEROUAC: I dunno . . . civil wars of my mind and memory . . .

STELLA: Should I ask Alex to come over?

KEROUAC: Let's have us a little drink, hah? . . . rop and dop, ligger lagger ligger . . .

STELLA: I wish you'd eat something . . .

KEROUAC: Wish I'd come sit sheepish at the table, huh? . . . be like the useless pioneer, the idiot in the wagon train who's got to be fed . . . doesn't do anything to help the men, nuthin' to please the women . . . *(Quieter)* . . . well, Stell, you knew what you were gettin' into . . .
(HE swigs from the bottle)

STELLA: If you're not going to eat, I won't bother to fix it. . . .

KEROUAC: You eat, you eat! Gotta keep up your strength to take care of the idiot invalids — hah!

STELLA: I'm not hungry . . . I think I'll go to bed, read maybe . . .

KEROUAC: . . . figured all I had to do was get a little home for me and Ma, read in the sun, pet my kitties. . . . Oh dammit . . . coulda been a *shaman*, coulda gone with Japh to Japan, been a big Zen Lunatic, sat under tangerine trees, shout in high voice at monk buddies, coulda lived in golden pavilion temple, coulda . . . coulda. . . . Yeah — "coulda." . . . Forty-seven years old, Stell, and all I got's my . . . rage . . .
(The lights start to dim)

STELLA: *(Tentative, shy)* . . . you have Gabrielle . . . and . . . and me . . .

KEROUAC: *(Absorbed in himself)* I've done irreparable harm — garradarable narm! . . . So lies a moral — don't light your lanterns too soon, it may be darker than you think . . .

STELLA: Jack . . . Jack, do —

KEROUAC: — irreparable harm —

STELLA: — do you . . . care for me? —

KEROUAC: — garradarable narm!

STELLA: Did you hear me, Jack?

KEROUAC: Huh?

STELLA: Can you . . . feel . . . affection for me?

KEROUAC: Whaddaya mean? Of course I do! . . . naturally, babe, naturally . . . *krissakes* — sure! *(HE wanders over to the window)* My dog Beauty died the night I discovered sex. They yelled it up to me — "ton chien est mort!" — at just that moment I was lying in bed finding out my tool had sensations in the tip . . .
(HE takes a deep swig, almost finishing the bottle)

137

STELLA: Jack, please . . . please take it easy . . . maybe if you go to bed, if you try to sleep —

KEROUAC: . . . Snake of the World . . . lifelong enemy . . .
(Lights dim further)
. . . put on the wrong regalia and think you're . . . Snake . . . coiled out there, inchin' up . . . hour by hour, all the ages of man . . . only five, four, three minutes from breakin' the crust . . . (HE *points agitatedly out of the window)* I — oh, Ruthie, *look!* LOOK! . . . blizzard's put a sheet of snow on the pane!

STELLA: *(Almost in tears)* Jacky . . . Jacky . . . it's — it's *Spring!*

KEROUAC: God! — I oughta call home! — Pa had to go to work in this muck! — I oughta call home — Maybe Pa's car'll be stuck . . . (HE *turns to* STELLA) Ruth . . . if we get to your house, Ruthie . . .
(STELLA starts to cry. SHE turns and runs into the back room. The lights dim further; stage now in semidarkness. KEROUAC finishes the bottle. The silhouette of a mountain peak appears on backdrop. Music under, low)

KEROUAC: Easy, Ruthie, *easy! (Laughs)* . . . sittin' on my hand like that! *(Jumps)* Huh, Pa — what? . . . it was them coaches not lettin' me smoke before breakfast, Pa, that's what I couldn't stand . . . you know I'm no quitter . . . *(Suddenly shudders, moans. Sound of bats' wings beating in the dark.* KEROUAC *jumps frantically, swoops and ducks)* Uh-oh . . . uh-oh, they're in the room . . . they're in the ROOM! . . . NO! . . . NO-O-O! Aii! . . . Aaoww! *(Moaning, almost inaudible)* . . . Oh mon Dieu, pourquoi Tu m'laisse faire malade comme

138

ça . . . Papa! Papa! aide mué! . . . Aw j'ai mal au coeur . . . j'ai mal au coeur . . .
(The figure of JAPHY, *in silhouette, appears in a crag of the mountain peak above stage)*
. . . 'shu malade . . . 'shu malade . . . Owaowaowao . . .

JAPHY: *(Looking toward top of the mountain peak)* Wow, heck, that's still a long way! The secret of climbing, Jacky, is Don't Think — just dance along —

KEROUAC: — Japh? . . . that you, Japh?

JAPHY: You're not sittin' in some Berkeley tea room now, Jacky. This here's the beginning and end of the world!

KEROUAC: O Japh! . . . Japh, you're the happiest little cat . . . I'm sure glad you're teachin' me all this . . .

JAPHY: *(Pointing)* Look over there — yellow aspens! *(Laughs happily)* Puts me in mind of a haiku:

"Talking about the literary life —
the yellow aspens."

(Takes off his pants and ties them around his waist, leaving him in shorts) Well — let's go! Another thousand feet. Gotta make it in a run or we'll never get there before nightfall.

KEROUAC: Whaddaya doin'?

JAPHY: Gettin' naked like an Indian! Whooo! Where we're goin', boy, you can bet your ass there won't be one human being. Ready?

KEROUAC: . . . too tired . . .

JAPHY: You can't come all this way and give up at the last minute! C'now — let's hurry!
(Sound of bats' wings begins again; music grows louder)

KEROUAC: *It's too high!*

JAPHY: Okay, boy! SEE — YA!
   (With an exuberant yell, JAPHY disappears. Sound of bats' wings louder)

KEROUAC: Japh! — *don't leave me here!* JAPH — Y — Y!
(HE *starts to whimper*) . . . don't think . . . mustn't think . . . rest . . . have to rest . . .
   (HE suddenly screams and ducks from the "swoop of a bat")
Aiii!! . . . Aaooww! . . . big slurry lips . . . beggars crappin' in burlap . . . dead vests . . . mémère . . . drug . . . Communist DRUG! Yawk photograph VLORK of the Rooster! . . . mud . . . steamin' mud . . . *pulling* . . . hot boiled *(screaming)* PORK BLOOD! . . . MÉMÈRE! MÉMÈRE!
   (Lights start to crisscross the stage)
. . . mountain . . . have to get . . . to mountain . . .
   (Lights turn into white spots that pitilessly scan the stage as KEROUAC tries to hide in a corner. HE cowers with head in hand)
(Whimpering and trembling) . . . Mon Pousse . . . Ti Mon Pousse . . . Mère de Dieu, priez pour nous . . . pêcheurs . . . maintenant et . . . a l'heure de notre mort . . .
   (The lights scan out once toward the audience, then immediately go out. Stage momentarily in darkness. Then a single shaft of light at the door. CODY appears, looking as he did at his first entrance, aged eighteen [act one, scene 2]. Music off)

CODY: *(Agitated; W. C. Fields accent)* For cryin' out loud, Jacky m'*boy*, how long you think that lil ol' pussy's gonna sit out there? Can't keep her goin' *all* by m'self, proud though I am of me comin' attractions! TIME, boy, *TIME!* Got to get on the ball, darlin', for a peaceful, understandin' of pure love between us, all hassles thrown *out!*

KEROUAC: *(weak)* Cody . . . Cody . . . I . . .

CODY: — no need to *worry,* adamantine boy —

KEROUAC: . . . where . . . where you been all this . . . time . . .

CODY: Been all over the world, Jacky . . . inveiglin' Indian wisdom, arms hangin' low, lazy eyes sayin', " 'Tis a pimp, son, a pimp hides at the secret heart of mystery . . ."

KEROUAC: . . . maybe if I just stay here, Cody . . . just try to be quiet and — kind . . .

CODY: — well, yass a'course, stare at the luminous Cross, watch the soft fud come creepin' over the sand — *I* understand, ol' buddy, understand com-*pletely.* It's like that alto man we heard last night — up to *him* to put down what everybody's feelin'. He starts the first chorus, rises to his fate, has to blow *equal* to it. All of a sudden somewhere in the middle he *gets* it — Time *stops!* He's fillin' empty space with the substance of our lives. Trumpet of the morning in America! . . . *(Pause)* And that's it. Cody, blank at last.

KEROUAC: . . . when . . . when will I see you again?
(Music builds in volume until final blackout)

CODY: See me?! We got the same flesh and bone . . . *(Pause. Gentle)* I saw, had a vision of you, handsome m'boy, walkin' across the top of America with your lantern-shadow —

KEROUAC: *(Crying)* — Cody . . . I pray you . . . get back safe . . .

141

CODY: Adios, you who watched the sun go down, smilin', at the rail, by my side. . . . We almost walked arm in arm. . . . Old fever Jack, good-bye. . . . *(Light out on* CODY*)*

KEROUAC: . . . Adios . . . Adios — King!

> *(*KEROUAC*'s body slumps to the floor. Lights up full: natural daylight.* KEROUAC *is lying on his back, eyes open in a glassy stare, palms turned upward, fingers locked.* HE *is dead. Freeze for a moment. Then blackout)*